I0820125

Praise for *Rain Date*

"*Rain Date* is a true American success story and a great example of saying 'the cream always rises to the top.' Nick was able to overcome huge adversities in life but instead of playing the victim card, used them to his advantage to become successful. Highly recommend reading for kids and adults of all ages."

—Jim Eberwine, retired NWS Meteorologist

"Nick Pittman has always been more than a meteorologist—he's a storyteller with heart, hustle, and a true love for the communities he serves. *Rain Date* pulls back the curtain on the grind, the grit, and the grace it takes to build trust in an era of fragmented attention and viral misinformation. It's funny, raw, inspiring—and most of all, it's real. This book belongs on the shelf of anyone who cares about local media, personal authenticity, or the human side of the weather business."

—Bill Murray, Chief Operating Officer, Alabama Weather Network

"Nick's story will be an inspiration for many readers. A living example of energy follows intention. What you think, you create. And if you love weather, it's a great peek behind the curtain on how weather forecasts are made and delivered. I highly recommend it!"

—Tony Pann, WBAL-TV Meteorologist

"In this deeply moving and inspiring memoir, Nor'Easter Nick Pittman takes readers on a journey through the storms of his youth—both literal and emotional. From a young student struggling to find his voice to a celebrated meteorologist captivating audiences with his passion and purpose. His story is a testament to resilience, hope, and the transformative power of educators. As a former TV/media student, Nor'Easter Nick offers a unique perspective on how mentorship, encouragement, and belief from just a few key teachers can forever change the trajectory of a young life. This book is not just a celebration of overcoming adversity; it's a heartfelt reminder that sometimes the biggest breaks in life come from being pushed to take a chance without seeing the opportunity for yourself. A must-read for teachers, students, and anyone who believes in the power of potential."

—Dr. Damiso A. Josey, CEO, The Empowerment Perspective Group

"A Horatio Alger tale for the digital age, *Rain Date: Unpredictable Lessons from My Life Forecasting the Weather* traces Nor'Easter Nick Pittman's remarkable rise from abandonment on the Jersey Shore to regional acclaim as a self-made meteorologist and media entrepreneur. Enduring childhood trauma and facing corporate giants along the way, Pittman's journey is powered by grit, determination, and relentless hope. This is a great American success story; proof that with perseverance and authenticity, anyone can build a life and legacy from humble beginnings. *Rain Date* is an inspiring tale of resilience, reinvention, and pursuing your dreams no matter the odds."

—Peter Galeta, Author, *The CDX Method*

"Reading *Rain Date* feels like sitting down with Nick himself. He turns life's toughest moments into stories full of grit, humor, and heart. From chasing storms in Brigantine to rebuilding after setbacks, his journey is honest, hopeful, and unforgettable—with his grandmother Bebe at the center of it all."

—Frank Chesky, General Counsel and VP, Hardrock International

"*Rain Date* is truly as unpredictable as the weather, but the outlook is bright and sunny for this read, even though Nick's pursuit of his professional life goal hits major turbulence. Yet, the uncertainty is matched with pure grit and serves as life lessons for all those, young and old, starting out with a dream and desire. You never get a sense that this guy is down and out in a time where being different from the norm can dampen one's outlook. It is those differences that resonate with the reader and allow for reflection as to the reader's own choices, and are relatable to each walk in life from each and every background. Filled with lessons and advice, this book should not be set aside or postponed for all those looking to start or reinvent their life or career path."

—Jeffrey S. Downs, Esquire, President and Owner, J. Downs Law

"*Rain Date* places you directly in Nick's shoes as he charts his course toward success. Like a storm system moving across varied terrain, his journey is at times bright with joy and at other moments shadowed by heartbreak. The story offers an insightful portrait of one of the finest men I've ever had the pleasure of knowing. Much like weathering the fiercest of tempests, Nick's perseverance shows us that success, in life and in business, can be achieved through hard work, steadfast dedication, and the will to rise above obstacles. *Rain Date* is both inspiring and uplifting, a testimony that clear skies often follow the storms we endure."

—Ben Luna, Meteorologist and Owner, Tennessee Valley Weather

RAIN DATE

RAIN DATE

Unpredictable Lessons from My Life Forecasting the Weather

Nick Pittman

Matt Holt Books
An Imprint of BenBella Books, Inc.
Dallas, TX

The events, locations, and conversations in this book while true, are re-created from the author's memory. However, the essence of the story, and the feelings and emotions evoked are intended to be accurate representations. In certain instances, names, persons, organizations, and places have been changed to protect an individual's privacy.

Matt Holt is an imprint of BenBella Books, Inc.
8080 N. Central Expressway
Suite 1700
Dallas, TX 75206
benbellabooks.com
Send feedback to feedback@benbellabooks.com

BenBella and *Matt Holt* are federally registered trademarks.

Printed in the United States of America
10 9 8 7 6 5 4 3 2 1

Library of Congress Control Number: 2025032868
ISBN 9781637748381 (hardcover)
ISBN 9781637748398 (electronic)

Editing by Katie Dickman
Copyediting by Scott Calamar
Proofreading by Michael Fedison and Denise Pangia
Text design and composition by Aaron Edmiston
Cover design by Brigid Peason
Cover image © Adobe Stock (map) / lesniewski
Cover photo by Beau Ridge
Printed by Versa Press

Rain Date *is dedicated to my late grandmother Charlotte Pittman. She took me in as a toddler, taught me everything I needed to know as a child, and prepared me for what life had in store for me. She instilled grit and determination. Our time together was cut short due to dementia but her lessons will always stick with me. I thank her for the person I am today.*

Contents

Preface xiii

Chapter One Storm Warning 1
Chapter Two Blizzard Dreams 9
Chapter Three Runaway Ride 15
Chapter Four Studio Beginnings 23
Chapter Five Groundhog Day 31
Chapter Six A Fork in the Forecast 35
Chapter Seven Storm Signals 45
Chapter Eight Final Days in Brigantine 51
Chapter Nine Heat Waves & Hard Times 57
Chapter Ten Growing Pains & Weather Games 63
Chapter Eleven Safe Harbor 69
Chapter Twelve Audition for a Dream 79
Chapter Thirteen Forecast: Bright Future 85
Chapter Fourteen Trial by Snow 93
Chapter Fifteen Lightning in a Bottle 99
Chapter Sixteen Holiday Storms & Station Shock 111
Chapter Seventeen Becoming Nor'Easter Nick 119
Chapter Eighteen Corporate Storm 131

Chapter Nineteen	North Star	137
Chapter Twenty	Chosen Ties	145
Chapter Twenty-One	A New Front	149
Chapter Twenty-Two	Forecast: Love	159
Chapter Twenty-Three	Tornado of Grief	163
Chapter Twenty-Four	Anchored in Love	169
Chapter Twenty-Five	Forecasting from Home	181
Chapter Twenty-Six	Back to the Green Screen	185
Chapter Twenty-Seven	Clouds of Uncertainty	191
Chapter Twenty-Eight	NorCast Is Born	195
Chapter Twenty-Nine	Weathering New Heights	201
Chapter Thirty	Networking in the Sky	209
Chapter Thirty-One	Weather Tips for Life	215
Chapter Thirty-Two	Shadows of the Past	219
	Acknowledgments	223

Preface

Writing this book is something I've wanted to do for many years now, but finding the time to actually sit down, collect my thoughts, and put pen to paper has been a real struggle. I'm all over the place. My life is a never-ending saga of covering severe weather, attending events, making in-person appearances, and trying to maintain personal relationships on top of everything else. I'm not going to lie—it can be *very* exhausting, but I know in the end it will all be worth it.

My story isn't very typical. There have been twists and turns from the start, and I've had to learn how to hurdle over mountains to deal with some massive obstacles along my journey. Honestly, though? I wouldn't trade anything I went through, because those experiences shaped me into the man I am today.

My name is Nick Pittman, I go by Nor'Easter Nick, and I've been broadcasting weather since 2010 to a niche market located east of Philadelphia and south of New York City. I have successfully transitioned from traditional television into the digital world using name recognition built on countless hours of hard work and devotion to become the absolute best I can be at my craft.

I've always been one to take the road less traveled; it's who I am and how I was brought up. In this book you will learn how I managed to start with nothing and end up being my own boss with a lucrative business and a fan base larger than I ever dreamed of. Most important to me? I get to practice what I love, where I love.

If you want to build your own empire down the road but either don't know where to start or are nervous to take the steps because of family issues or maybe a lack of support from your peers, trust me, no matter *what* your situation, you *can* do this. I know it may sound cliché, but you've got the tools to make any of your dreams possible. There was a time in my life when I thought it impossible to get to my goal, but through determination I was able to beat the system and stack the cards in my favor. The lessons in this book will teach you how to do the same.

Chapter One

STORM WARNING

Good morning, New Jersey: Nor'Easter Nick here with today's forecast. We're looking at a hot day with mostly cloudy skies and strong winds . . .

—Nick Pittman, SNJ Today

It's impossible to live in New Jersey and not think about the weather. A lot. In the summer, we bask in saltwater breezes, and in the winter we muddle through snowstorms and floods. Weather affects our life, from little daily decisions to seasonal big ones. The dramatic weather terrified me as a child, then fascinated me, then became my lifeline.

I've been forecasting the local weather for over fifteen years now, and the challenge never gets dull. Even with the billions of dollars in technology meteorologists have at our disposal, there are wild swings that we don't see coming. Or, sometimes we do, but we're helpless to get our viewers and audience out of harm's way because it's impossible to connect with every single person that could be impacted. In that way, weather forecasting is a lot like life. Especially life as I've known it.

But when I was in my mid-twenties, during the summer of 2016, I thought I finally had everything figured out. I was engaged to a wonderful man, I lived in my favorite place, and I had my dream career as the chief meteorologist at a small Southern New Jersey news station. I was part of the founding team at SNJ Today, and four years in we still had a start-up mentality. We fought hard for our slice of the news market, and the challenges and successes had bonded us like a little family.

"Good morning, Megan," I said to our news director. Megan was a true newswoman who never let her own opinions or bias slip into her reporting. She'd been a producer at my first news station job, WMGM-TV 40, and was one of the first people I suggested for our team when we launched SNJ Today. "I got your email and, yes, count us in for drinks tomorrow night."

"Excellent," she said with a smile. "Hey, how was your commute? Any debris in the roads?"

"Not too much," I said.

She frowned.

We'd all driven home the night before in a thunderous downpour. My commute took an hour longer than usual, but I found dramatic storms thrilling. I hadn't always felt that way. In fact, just the opposite: One of my earliest childhood memories is the terror I felt when a storm rolled in.

I was living with my grandmother in her big house on the water in Brigantine on the Jersey Shore. My parents had abandoned me as a toddler, and my grandmother's home had been my own ever since.

My bedroom on the second floor had six windows facing the bay. It was my favorite spot in the house. I would look out at the water, watching the sailboats as they passed by the sign on the dock across the way reading "No wake" in big painted letters. I imagined being on one of those boats, feeling as free as the seagulls that circled overhead. With the windows open, I could hear them squawking, and to me that was the ultimate sound, not just of summer but of home. One day when I was looking out across the bay, my boyhood imagination running wild, the sky changed in an instant. Dark clouds rolled in, and it got deathly silent. The winds picked up, and the more forceful gusts made the house shake.

My grandmother came running in. "Nick, close those windows," she said. I'd never seen her move so fast. By that time, the silence was replaced by the roll of thunder in the distance. In retrospect, I should have helped her secure the windows. Instead, I sat there feeling confused and scared as she lowered all the shades. Even though moments ago I had been completely lost in thought gazing at the sun-dappled water, the room was now dark as night.

More thunder rumbled and a crack of nearby lightning lit up the room. And then, complete darkness. The house lost electricity. To my young mind, with such limited experience, it felt like the world was ending. It probably would have been terrifying to any little kid, but it also triggered a memory that came back to me whenever I felt unsafe. I didn't remember much about the time before living with my grandmother, the years when I lived with my mother. But in moments of stress, I had flashbacks to being held underwater in a bathtub by a person I couldn't name or place. But the terror I felt left a lasting imprint.

When I was little, every rumble of thunder sent me scrambling under the bed, where I'd stay until the skies fell silent again. That became my go-to hiding place during every storm that followed. One day, my grandmother gave me a book about weather. I can't recall the title, but I devoured every page—and then asked for more. Through reading, I slowly began to understand the storms that once terrified me.

I learned that lightning wasn't a cosmic punishment, just a natural reaction to the forces inside a thundercloud. Here's how it works: Strong winds within a storm cloud push water droplets upward, where temperatures are much colder. Some of these droplets freeze into ice. As the ice particles collide with water droplets and other bits of ice, electrons are knocked loose, creating an imbalance of electrical charge within the cloud. The top becomes positively charged, the bottom negatively charged. When the difference in charge becomes too great, the cloud discharges that energy as lightning.

Thunder, the sound that used to shake me to my core, isn't an angry roar from the heavens. It's the result of air superheating along the lightning's path—hotter than the surface of the sun in an instant—causing that air to expand rapidly and create a shock wave: the boom we hear as thunder.

Understanding the science didn't just ease my fear. It gave me direction. What once sent me hiding under the bed became the thing that pulled me out from under it. I knew then what I wanted to be: a meteorologist.

I started every day at the SNJ Today station by logging into my broadcast equipment.

To put together the temperature forecast, I pulled up real-time temperatures and checked them against the map to see where we were versus where we were *supposed* to be (based on forecast models from the day before). From that, I could extrapolate to where we'd be in the future. If it was warmer by a couple degrees, that would usually apply to the upcoming few days because the model overestimated or underestimated how things would play out. It was the same process with evaluating cloud cover: I looked at different layers of the atmosphere, read the temperature and humidity, and assessed how that would impact the near future. I would look at models going out a few days, see where storm systems were, and what the air mass was looking like.

One morning my phone pinged with a text from our CEO, Frank DiMauro. "Can you take a break and meet me out back in the parking lot?"

I thought that was an odd request, but I texted back that I would be there in ten minutes. I had the utmost respect for Frank. The station wouldn't exist without him. He was a highly experienced, brilliant executive who'd taken a significant pay cut from his previous position to lead the team at SNJ Today. He had a passion for news—especially news that was produced to serve the local community. Frank was such an interesting person with all sorts of talents, an intellectual who also worked on cars. A true jack-of-all-trades! No day was complete unless I stopped by his office to ponder the mysteries of the world before heading down to the studio to do the news. Frank handpicked each of us to be on the team, and he was the glue that held us all together.

Outside, I spotted Frank waiting in one of his many Mercedes collectibles. He waved and leaned over, opening the passenger door for me. I climbed in.

"What's going on?" I said. "Is everything OK?"

Frank shook his head, and my stomach sank. The station had been having money issues for a while now. From day one, the giant cable conglomerate Comcast gave us a hard time, blocking our use of a primary channel and forcing us into a tenuous financial situation buying airtime from a third party.

"Nick, I wanted to let you know we're closing down the station. I'm sorry."

"I don't know what to say." I responded in a way that sounded like I had just been punched in the gut.

Maybe I should have known. After all, I'd been through this before. The last station I'd worked at—the one that gave me my start in broadcasting at age seventeen—had shuttered after Comcast bought it. And now it looked like history was repeating itself.

"What is there to say?" Frank shook his head. "We tried everything to make this company successful. I know I made some mistakes but—"

"We've been lucky to have you," I said, and I meant it. No one could blame Frank. I felt that way about our entire team. We'd all worked hard, and we'd succeeded in becoming a beloved local resource with a loyal audience. But after eight years as a meteorologist, I was starting to realize being good at what I did might not be enough. It was all about competing for airtime and advertising dollars. And we had no shot in the age of corporate monoliths like Comcast.

When I got home that night, Brandon knew something was bothering me before I even sat down for dinner. But he also knew me well enough not to push, knowing that I'd tell him what was going on when I was ready. We'd been together for almost five years—since our very first date. I proposed a few months prior, and we were in the thick of wedding planning.

"Frank told me the station is shutting down. No one else knows yet."

Brandon's brown eyes widened, and he filled my glass with sparkling water. I don't drink, but in that moment I wished I had an easy way to take my mind off the bad news. Instead, my thoughts were racing. It was my personality to tackle a problem head-on, to take charge and fix it. But this situation was out of my hands. And I wished I didn't know about it so far in advance since I couldn't change it, and I also couldn't tell anyone about it. It was like seeing a massive storm on the radar and wondering how rough it would be to ride it out. Wondering what the aftermath would look like. But with weather, I had a lot of science and technology to help me make good estimates. To plan ahead. Here, I was flying blind.

"He doesn't want me to tell anyone else at the station."

Brandon nodded. "This is rough. I'm sorry. I know how much you've invested in the station."

Joining SNJ Today meant giving up my financial safety net. For the decade before joining the station, ever since I was a freshman in high school, I'd been working at the local ShopRite. I started as a cart pusher and worked my way up to manager. Even after I got my first break in television weather, I kept my ShopRite job. But when SNJ Today offered me the chief meteorology position, I could no longer do both. Quitting ShopRite had been a huge leap of faith.

Brandon's phone chimed with a text. It was hard not to say something about it. We had mutually agreed to a no-phones-at-dinner policy. But I'd broken the rule a few times myself lately.

"It's the woman from the wedding venue," he said. "We have to make a decision on that tent."

Not this again. We were having an outdoor wedding, and the optional tent cost $500. I felt it was something we could ask for at the last minute if needed, but Brandon wanted it locked in. I felt his fear of rain on our wedding day was irrational. He was marrying a weather forecaster! I would know if we needed to make arrangements the day before. But he didn't want to have to scramble for a plan B.

"It's our wedding day we're talking about here," Brandon said. "There's no rain date. So I want them prepared to set up for any conditions. Just look at it as rain insurance."

I didn't mind spending money when we needed to, but if there was one thing I didn't need insurance for, it was the weather. There were very few weather-related surprises for me.

It was the one area of life where I was always prepared. And I worked hard to make it that way.

High temperature: 81°F **Low temperature:** 66°F
Conditions: Breezy with building clouds

Today, low pressure offshore created a sharp pressure gradient, leading to strong gusts from the southeast. It reminded me that not every storm announces itself with thunder and lightning—sometimes it's a slow build. A shift in wind. A gut feeling. Just like in life, storms don't always arrive when expected, but you still have to be ready.

—Nick's weather journal

Chapter Two

BLIZZARD DREAMS

This one will go down in the record books. More than a foot of snow is already on the ground in some areas with 22 inches reported in others. And the snow is expected to continue for hours. Buckle in for a nor'easter, folks! Heavy snow and strong winds are creating whiteout conditions with snow accumulations of 18–30 inches expected by evening. Please, stay off the roads.

—Jim Cantore, The Weather Channel, January 1996

I lived with my grandmother growing up, just the two of us, on a small island over the bridge from Atlantic City in a town called Brigantine. I loved the smell of salt water and the calming breeze off the ocean. I found the climate soothing and uplifting and inspiring. Brigantine is a special place, a town that is still the home of my heart.

My grandmother's three-story home on the back bay was a front-row seat to a lot of dramatic weather. One day in January 1996, I wandered down into the kitchen early in the morning and saw nothing but white outside the windows. Snow! A lot of it. I couldn't see the sky or the water, just a whirl of flakes. At five years old, I'd never seen anything like it.

"Bebe," I said, running up the stairs to my grandmother's third-floor bedroom. "It's snowing."

Clearly, this was not news to her. It was early, but she was already dressed to the nines. She always cared about her appearance. Not a single strand of her curly blond hair was ever out of place, her big eyes always perfectly lined and shadowed. She didn't like her eye color so she wore hazel contacts—something I didn't learn until much later. It only added to my sense that Bebe had everything under control at all times. Don't like your eye color? Just change it. In the winter, she never left the house without one of her oversized fur coats. The daughter of an Italian South Philly bookie and a Russian Jewish immigrant, she was as old-school as they came.

"It certainly is," she said, ushering me down to the living room. "Let's watch the news and see what's what."

I knew it had to be serious if Bebe was willing to sit around watching TV first thing in the morning. She had a very get-up-and-go approach to life. But that day we sat side by side on her pink, floral, 1960s-era wraparound sofa. The living room had half a dozen huge windows, and the snow was so high it covered the bottom halves of the panes.

I settled next to my grandmother while she flipped through the channels. I'd never seen the news on in the morning before—it was something we watched together after dinner.

"They've preempted all the morning shows," she told me, explaining this was when the news broke to replace the game shows that normally aired at that time. I had no idea a news broadcast could do that, and it seemed all powerful to me.

"We're going to cut to Jim Cantore over at The Weather Channel," the news anchor said, going to a live shot of a weatherman broadcasting in the extreme conditions somewhere just north of New York City. He was dressed in a blue coat and wore a Weather Channel knit cap. He had prominent dark eyebrows and didn't seem to mind the wind and snow whipping all around him. In fact, he was smiling and spoke excitedly.

"In a blizzard, you have to have wind," he was saying. "You don't necessarily have to have snow falling at a crazy pace, or falling at that time at all. But the wind has to pick up previously fallen snow on the ground and blow it around so you don't have visibility. What we have today is big winds and the falling snow at the same time, so we have whiteout conditions. This is pretty extraordinary stuff." A gust blew off his hat and carried it away. "I would chase that down except, as you can see, I wouldn't get very far." The camera operator panned down to show the snow drifts as high as his thighs. "So you folks at home can imagine how it feels to be outside in these conditions. What we have here isn't just any storm: It's a nor'easter and blizzard wrapped up in one."

I was in awe of every word he said. Things like "arctic high-pressure system" and "precipitation." I memorized them, building a script I could replay in my mind alone in my room at night if the storm continued.

Cantore didn't just seem to know a lot about weather; he seemed to be enjoying it. I'd never seen a grown man having so much fun.

"Let's go outside!" I said.

"What a good idea!" Bebe was always up for an adventure. But as soon as I made the suggestion, I wanted to take it back. The air felt charged, and while it wasn't as scary as a thunder and lightning storm, I felt the same sense of not being in control. I didn't like that feeling. At my young age, I'd already experienced it far too often.

But I bundled up in my puffy winter coat, Bebe helped me into my snow boots, and we ventured out into the backyard. The snow was so high I could barely walk, and some of the drifts were double my height.

I was enamored.

"Beautiful, right?" Bebe asked, her fur dragging in the snow.

Absolutely—it was stunning. Honestly, it left me in a trance. What struck me most was how huge and powerful the snow looked blanketing everything, yet when I scooped some up, the delicate crystals melted away in seconds if I held them too long.

With the landscape buried, it was disorienting to look around and not see any of the familiar shrubs or footpaths. It seemed very possible, if not likely, that they were gone forever.

"What's going to happen with all this snow?" I asked.

"Well, we can shovel it. But also, if we're patient, the snow will melt, and before you know it, the lawn will be green again."

I was unconvinced, and the winds started whipping the snow around to the point where I couldn't see anything. We rushed back inside, where I shed my soaked outerwear and reclaimed my spot on the couch while Bebe made hot chocolate.

Bebe put on the local news. We learned that Newark airport was shut down. There was no train service running in or out of New York City. In Elizabeth, New Jersey, the state unemployment office collapsed under the weight of the snow. Entire neighborhoods were losing power, and to prepare for that possibility in ours, my grandmother went around the house setting out candles to use later if we fell victim to the same fate.

I switched back to The Weather Channel, wanting to see what Jim Cantore was doing. He stood in lashing winds on a deserted street punctuated with blinking traffic lights. The snow was blowing so hard the broadcast appeared as if it had been shot on grainy film.

"Look at the drifts we have here!" he said, putting a yardstick in a mountain of snow. "Just incredible!" The wind whipped around and his voice rose with excitement. Having just experienced a fraction of what he was dealing with, I could imagine how he felt. It must have been thrilling to be out there in front of the camera telling everyone what was happening. "Look at how the visibility drops when the winds start gusting at thirty to forty miles an hour. Oh!"

The camera suddenly panned away from him, then back. "The winds just knocked one of my cameramen down," he said. But the winds didn't seem to make him lose a step. Watching him, I got the sense that he not only understood the weather—and could predict it—he'd also found a way to be undaunted by it. At the time, I couldn't explain the feeling of hope that watching Jim Cantore gave me. But it was the sense that he could weather any storm.

My grandmother always encouraged me and seemed to have a can-do attitude, and Cantore seemed to embody her approach to life standing tall in the middle of a blizzard.

I was hooked. From that day on, The Weather Channel was my TV viewing of choice, and Jim Cantore was my superhero. Watching him day after day, a road map for my life took shape.

"I want to be a weatherman," I told my grandmother. I don't think she was surprised at all. She just nodded, as if it made perfect sense to her that her five-year-old grandson had already set his sights on a career.

"Then that's what you'll do," she said.

Was it that simple? I was only five. If my grandmother said I could make it happen, then I believed her.

"How?" I asked—the first of so many questions. But she had endless patience.

"You learn as much as you can. You try as hard as you can. And you *keep* trying."

"But what if I can't do it?" I said, unwilling to accept that something could actually work out. Even though I was safe with my grandmother, the earliest years of my life had taught me that the world was a chaotic place. Things could turn dangerous at a moment's notice. I had learned to hope for the best but prepare for the worst.

"Nick," she said. "Just never give up. If you keep trying, you always have a chance to succeed."

I hoped she was right. The idea of being a weatherman seemed too good to be true. But as long as I was under her roof, I'd have the courage to try.

High temperature: 31°F **Low temperature:** 19°F
Conditions: Heavy snow with strong winds

Blizzard conditions today created whiteout conditions and deep snow drifts. Watching the snow swirl felt overwhelming but also oddly beautiful. In meteorology, blizzards aren't just defined by snowfall—they require sustained winds and reduced visibility. It's not about how much you can measure—it's about what you can't see ahead. Just like in life, it's not always the storm itself that's hardest... it's the feeling of being lost in it. But with the right guidance, you learn how to stand tall in the wind.

—Nick's weather journal

Chapter Three

RUNAWAY RIDE

Tons of sunshine with highs topping out in the upper 70s, abnormally warm for this time of year. Great start to the day, looks like things could turn a little stormy later on as pressure drops.

While my hometown of Brigantine was an amazing little place with tons of beautiful views of beaches and the high-rises of Atlantic City, it wasn't exactly the shopping mecca of South Jersey. We had to travel off the island for pretty much everything we needed.

Whether it was for food shopping or some retail therapy, we took a twenty-minute drive onto the mainland. This was a trip Bebe and I would make once a week, and I really looked forward to it. I swear I was born as a sixty-year-old man—yes, I actually really enjoyed going grocery shopping.

Every now and then, we would go with my grandmother's best friend, Julie. We had the best times together. She was someone I would spend hours on the phone with, talking about politics and world affairs.

Yes. I know. I was only a kid, but at that time those were the things that interested me most. We always had the most interesting conversations, and to this day, I miss her a lot.

Bebe enjoyed Julie coming along so she didn't have to drive—I swear that woman always had a reason for everything.

One day, Bebe came down the steps, visibly disappointed, and told me: "Julie can't make it today. She has to take Wolfie to the vet. I guess it's just us today, Nicky."

I was disappointed, too, but I was still happy to get out of the house and go on our mini adventure together.

We hopped in her 1998 Celica. She would go back and forth from large Cadillacs to small sports cars. It never made a lick of sense to me, but she liked the car, and that's all that mattered.

I remember that week she had some issues with it, but nothing bad enough to prevent her from driving it. A mechanic friend suggested she not take it out until the issues were taken care of, but she was a very stubborn woman who rarely took anyone's advice but her own—so off we went.

After so many years of going to the Absecon ShopRite, my grandmother made friends with everyone—from the store manager to the self-check clerks. It would take us a good two hours to get through the store after her endless conversations with these people.

I was particularly eager to get home on this day because it was beautiful, and I figured I could get a couple hours of bike riding in—one of my favorite pastimes when I was a kid.

We placed what felt like a year's worth of groceries on the conveyor belt, and I rushed to the end of the lane to bag everything up neatly. It was like a game to me.

Bebe liked double paper—no plastic, because she felt it was bad for the environment. I packed everything as neatly as I could and placed the bags in the cart.

We left the store, waving goodbye to all of the workers, and walked to the car. After putting the bags in the small trunk, we buckled up and got ready to take the half-hour journey home.

It wasn't even two seconds after Bebe turned the key to the ignition when I felt a violent jolt and lost track of where we were or what was happening. All I can remember is a loud bang, screeching tires, and wood planks all over the windshield.

Within moments, we realized the car was out of control, and there was no stopping it. Bebe did her best to navigate around countless cars that were in our way. We blew through stop signs and red lights as we made our way onto Route 30, the major highway that leads back to Brigantine.

I was terrified. I saw my life flash before my eyes.

Is this how it ends? I asked myself.

There was no stopping this car. Bebe slammed on the brakes as hard as possible, stomping the pedal into the floor, but nothing helped. The engine wouldn't stop.

With tears running down both of our faces, we believed this once-ordinary trip to the grocery store was now going to end our lives. Suddenly, a sense of calm came over me as I had an idea—

What if I turned the key? Would that stop the car? I thought.

I reached over to the ignition, turned the key, and suddenly the car started to slow until it eventually came to a stop. Bebe was able to steer it over to the side of the road.

We unbuckled our seat belts and raced out the door to survey the damage. The car was totaled. The hood was bent up over itself and had cracked the windshield. The entire front half of the car was crinkled like a cheap soda can—but none of that mattered since we were alive and walked away from it unharmed.

After an investigation, it was revealed that the transmission failed, which caused the car to get stuck at high speeds. Bebe never drove again after that day.

It took her a long time to even want to get back in a car as a passenger. I feel like that day took an important part of my grandmother's life away. She absolutely loved driving before the accident. We would go everywhere, and she always looked forward to going on adventures. She wasn't really a fan of short trips to the grocery store or mall—she'd often cajole friends to take her around—but rather preferred long-distance driving. It was exciting to her. However, I understood how the guilt she felt about almost killing us could have led to her aversion to driving again.

Because we still had to get around—we had errands to run and lives to live—we turned to public transportation. I don't think Bebe had ever been on a city bus in her life, but now it was her only option if we were going to stay active.

For me, it was exciting. It was a chance to try something new and see a different perspective of life. We were lucky that the bus stop was only two blocks from our house.

The 501 came every hour at fifteen past. It traveled the entire length of Brigantine and went into Atlantic City, where we could connect to the vast network of buses that would take us anywhere we wanted to go.

We could get to Philadelphia, New York, Cape May, and the mall. All the places we were so used to driving to were reachable by bus, and now she didn't have to worry about getting into an accident. Granted, it was a little more time-consuming, but she felt safe, and I think that gave her peace of mind.

I sat there on every bus trip observing everything—the details of the bus, the driver, the other passengers, and the conversations being held. I soaked it all in like a sponge.

Over time, I developed a genuine love for public transportation—especially riding the bus. I looked forward to it every day. The more my face became familiar, the more the NJ Transit drivers opened up to me. I was always curious, always watching, always learning. Eventually, some of the drivers began giving me pieces of their uniform—small tokens that meant the world to me. I wore them with pride.

My interest didn't stop when I stepped off the bus. At home, I built an elaborate bus-themed board game, complete with routes, transfers, and delays. I memorized every South Jersey schedule I could find, learning each stop and time like a second language. I read transit maps like they were novels and spent hours tracing routes just for fun. Any time I had the chance to ride a new line, I jumped on it—literally.

Sometimes, passengers even asked me for directions, thinking I worked for NJ Transit. I always had an answer.

Along the way, I made some lasting friendships—people who still remember the little kid who showed up every week in an oversized uniform shirt, beaming with excitement. It means a lot to stay connected with them. Not many remember me that way, but those who do hold a special place in my story.

I feel like Bebe loved the buses even more than I did because, as I look back on that period, I can see it was a kind of babysitting service. She could put her feet up, read magazines, and relax while the drivers looked after me.

Going into Center City Philadelphia was my grandmother's favorite pastime. Before the accident we drove into the city nearly every Saturday. She'd visit her jeweler friends, and we'd walk around the fashion district—at the time called the Gallery.

After she stopped driving, it weighed on her that she might no longer be able to do those things, but we found a bus to take us there! The 551 departed from Atlantic City, and within ninety minutes, it dropped us off right at Market Street in Philadelphia.

We did that trip so many times. I liked it because it was a different kind of bus—a bigger one designed for long distances. It was nice to see the variety of the fleet.

My love of buses took a back seat to a new love of trains during a busy summer weekend in 2000. The Atlantic City Expressway was backed up as far as the eye could see, and the travel time into Philadelphia nearly doubled.

Instead of canceling our day trip, we decided to walk a few blocks from the bus terminal to the train station and board the Gambler's Express for the first time. I was immediately enthralled by the lights, sounds, and speed of the train.

The first person we encountered on the trip was a young woman with curly, strawberry-blond hair.

"You are just too adorable," she said to me, looking at my bus driver uniform.

"My name is Fran. I'm the conductor. Are you going into Philly with us today?"

I didn't immediately reply with a verbal answer but shook my head up and down as if it were going to fall off my neck.

"Yes, we are. This is our first time. This is my grandmother, Charlotte, and I'm Nicky," I finally replied.

It was the best trip I had ever experienced, and I was hooked from that moment on. At the end of the trip, Fran invited us to come back anytime we wanted—it was an invitation we would accept many, many times.

Riding the train to Philly and back became our weekend adventure for several years. Fran gave me pieces of the conductor's uniform over time, and she actually let me help the crew by taking tickets, making announcements, and giving the weather forecast over the loudspeaker. I was in heaven.

On my ninth birthday in 2001, Fran asked me if I wanted to ride up on the locomotive with the engineer. It was like a dream come true.

I'm not going to lie—at first I was a bit intimidated by the engineer, Bob, because of his gruff looks. But once we started talking, we hit it off instantly.

Climbing up on a gigantic, loud, vibrating piece of metal with three thousand horsepower that traveled eighty miles an hour through the pines was incredible. I wanted more and more.

The cherry on top for me was connecting with Bob on a deeply personal level. I didn't have a father figure in my life, and he checked that box for me over the years. He had had a rough childhood, enduring all kinds of trauma.

Our stories were very similar, and he became someone I could confide in. I've now known Bob for over twenty years and we remain close friends. He is retired these days, but we still get together and laugh about old memories.

I look back on that car accident in 1998, and I'm grateful for what happened as a result. I made lifelong friends who helped me grow, but I also developed a deep passion for a hobby that has allowed me to flourish outside of work.

High temperature: 79°F **Low temperature:** 61°F
Conditions: Calm morning, isolated thunderstorms by evening

Today started crystal clear—light winds, blue skies—but by afternoon, isolated storms popped up from an unstable air mass. That's the thing about pop-up storms: You don't always see them coming, but sometimes they change everything. Like a failed transmission that reroutes your life, not every storm is a setback. Some carry you straight into new passions, new people, and new purpose.

—Nick's weather journal

Chapter Four

STUDIO BEGINNINGS

Good morning, Brigantine! My name is Nick Pittman, and I'm gonna tell you about the weather every day! We've got clouds and sun mixing, some rain possible later so—I hope you brought your umbrella to school!

—Nick's first BRIGANTINE NEWS NETWORK broadcast

I got my start in broadcast weather at a very young age. I was obsessed in every single way. I would spend hours at night and on weekends watching my favorite forecasters on TV. I'd listen to every word they said and observe their mannerisms, knowing I wanted to be in their shoes one day.

What I find ironic is that the very company I thought would one day end my TV career actually helped kick-start it at Brigantine Elementary. By the time I was in third grade, the city struck a deal with Comcast to build a state-of-the-art television studio in an empty storage space on the second floor. My homeroom teacher, Mrs. Levitt, knew I had a fascination with TV and encouraged me to take the class as a "special."

She walked me down the hall to the studio to introduce me to Ms. Kaufman, who was in charge of the program. When the door swung open, it revealed an awe-inspiring collection of cameras, TV monitors, audio equipment, and a bright neon-green wall.

"Hi, Nicky! Mrs. Levitt tells me you want to be on TV one day . . ."

I was doing my best to pay attention and be respectful, but everything in the room distracted me. I couldn't help but envision myself standing in front of the green wall, making silly motions to explain Brigantine's daily weather.

"Absolutely! I've been practicing for a long time, and when I'm older and out of school, I want to be on 6abc," I told her confidently.

"Well, this will be the perfect place for you, then. How would you feel about auditioning to work on our morning show? I think you'd fit right in."

The look of joy on my face could have been seen from the moon. I couldn't stop smiling.

"That would be incredible! I'll see you tomorrow!" I said as Mrs. Levitt led me back to her classroom.

I couldn't wait to get home to tell Bebe that not only did we have a shiny new television studio in town, but I also had the chance to finally do what I'd been dreaming of. From that moment on, I became even more obsessed with weather and media. I made sure to watch intently each evening at six fifteen when the forecast came on.

I wanted to be just like Hurricane Schwartz or Dan Skeldon when I grew up!

Bebe was a big fan of Philadelphia news, having grown up in the city, but she often flipped over to NBC40 for the local scoop. I made sure my news consumption was as balanced as possible, especially since the weather varied so much between Philly and the Jersey Shore.

When it came time to audition for the morning show, I was nervous. My palms were sweaty, and I had butterflies in my stomach. But as soon as Ms. Kaufman looked at me and said, "Nicky, you've got it," my anxiety disappeared.

"We'll work on some delivery issues, but you're solid, and I think you've got a bright future in this field," she added.

You could have told me I'd won a million dollars, and I wouldn't have been more excited. This was my big chance to practice my craft and develop my skills so I could one day live my dream.

I made it a point to get to school an hour early every day to study the forecast, create my graphics, and practice what I was going to say. I wanted to be the authority on all things weather. Hundreds of students and faculty were watching my every move!

In the beginning, I was so nervous that I wrote a full script on giant poster boards each morning. One of the other kids in the studio would hold them up just out of the camera's view.

Over time, I abandoned that method. Within three months, I transitioned to memorizing bullet points and learning how to talk on the fly.

Ms. Kaufman was a former NBC40 reporter with years of experience. She was incredibly patient and worked with me to improve my delivery. By spring, I was completely self-sufficient, and my presentations looked polished.

I spent most of my days in the studio, often skipping lunch to hang out with Ms. Kaufman. We'd discuss television and her experiences in the industry. I shared my dreams and ambitions, and she was always supportive.

Knowing her background, I asked her about Dan Skeldon, NBC40's meteorologist, whom I watched every night with Bebe.

"I've known Dan for quite a few years. I'm sure he'd love to visit us and see our studio. Let me see what I can arrange," she said.

That afternoon, she sent him an email. I couldn't stop thinking about it as I watched Dan on the screen later that evening.

The next day, I showed up at the studio ten minutes earlier than usual, hoping for good news.

"Good morning, Ms. Kaufman! Soooo, did Dan get back to you?" I asked, far too excited for 6:50 in the morning.

"Not yet, but don't worry. I'm sure we'll hear something soon."

I'd be lying if I said I wasn't at least a little disappointed. I wanted an answer immediately. I was an impatient kid—and, to this day, I'm an impatient adult. Waiting has never been my strong suit.

I went about my day as usual. The next day came and went. Still nothing. I was starting to think I should just forget about it. Dan was obviously a very busy man, or maybe the email got lost. Maybe he didn't even check his email. Who knows?

I was bummed, but I moved on and filled that void with more practice.

It was an unusually cold spring day, and we actually had snow in the forecast. Instead of going outside for recess, we stayed in and watched a show.

"Nick Pittman, please report to Mr. DiGiovanni's office," a loud voice announced over the intercom.

All eyes were on me—and not in a good way. Whispers floated around the room as I stood up. Mr. D—our vice principal and the school's official disciplinarian—had just called my name.

But why?

I was the straight-A kid. The rule follower. The one teachers used as an example. I couldn't think of a single thing I'd done wrong.

Still, my palms were sweaty as I made my way down the hallway. My footsteps echoed louder than usual. When I reached his office, I paused, heart pounding—and knocked on the door.

"Mr. Pittman, come in. Have a seat," he said.

He looked at me with no emotion, like he was about to grill me for leaking top-secret government data to the Russians.

"Do you know why I called you down here?"

"Honestly, Mr. D, no, I don't," I replied nervously.

Suddenly, the scowl on his face vanished, replaced by a big smile. The tension in my back instantly eased.

"A little birdie told me you wanted to meet Dan Skeldon. Well, Ms. Kaufman heard back from him today, and we're planning to have him visit us next Tuesday. I need your help getting ready for the visit."

It was as though a billion-pound weight had been lifted off my chest—and I'd won the lottery at the same time. My fear turned to elation.

Dan Skeldon was coming to visit ME?! This was the best day of my life. I couldn't wait to go home and tell Bebe. We watched the news that night with an extra dose of excitement.

Normally, I longed for the weekend, wanting it to go as slowly as possible so I could enjoy all my time with Bebe and riding buses and trains. But this weekend? I wanted it to pass by like a rocket so I could get to Tuesday.

That Monday, I spent the entire day preparing the studio, making sure everything was absolutely perfect. To me, Dan was the most famous person we were ever going to have visit our little school, and I wanted to impress him.

"Nicky, I think you should interview Dan on the set. We'll run it as a special on Friday. Come up with some questions. If you need help, let me know," Ms. Kaufman said.

I knew exactly what I was going to do, and I was determined to make it the best interview ever. I wanted to make Ms. Kaufman proud. I wanted to make Bebe proud. Nothing was going to get in my way.

T-minus twelve hours until Dan gets here!

That Tuesday morning, I woke up so early it felt like I hadn't gone to bed at all. By 4 AM, I was going over my questions, picking out my outfit, and trying to make my hair look just right.

For all I knew, this could be the first day of my TV career.

After the morning announcements wrapped up, we received a call on the station phone. It was Mr. D. Dan was only ten minutes away. I rushed down to his office to meet Dan at the school entrance.

I saw the NBC40-painted Jeep pull up on Lafayette Avenue. Within minutes, a tall, slender man stepped out from the driver's side. His long overcoat made him look seven feet tall.

This is it, I thought.

I stood in the doorway and greeted Dan with a gigantic smile.

"Hi, Dan! My name is Nicky. My grandmother and I watch you every night. I think you're great! Thank you so much for coming to our school!"

I barely came up for air, I was so enthusiastic.

He smiled and said, "I've heard so many good things about you. What you're doing is impressive. You know, my love of weather started when I was about your age, back when Hurricane Gloria hit New England. I'm proud of you for being this zealous so young."

I led him from the middle school over to the elementary school, and we chatted about his TV career during the short walk.

I was so proud to show him what we'd built and what we did, but I was nervous too—I idolized him, and now he was right beside me, geeking out over the weather with me.

When we walked into the studio, Ms. Kaufman greeted us warmly. They spent a few minutes catching up in the control room while I prepared the interview set.

Dan unbuttoned his coat and sat beside me at the desk as I fumbled through my papers with my poorly written questions.

"You're on in 3 . . . 2 . . . 1 . . ." the floor director announced, pointing to me.

"Good morning, Brigantine. Nick Pittman here with NBC40 chief meteorologist Dan Skeldon," I said confidently.

The interview felt natural. We talked about his career, his passion for meteorology, and we even fantasized about major blizzards. He asked me some questions, too, making it feel more like a conversation than an interview.

As we wrapped up, I asked him a question that would change my life.

"Dan, I've always wanted a fun nickname like Hurricane Schwartz. What do you think?"

Without hesitation, he replied, "Nor'Easter Nick."

I loved it. It had a ring to it. Nor'Easter Nick. That name would become my identity for the rest of my life.

Before he left, Dan gave me NBC40 memorabilia and pointers on forecasting and using the green screen. He chuckled when I showed him how I'd been taking *his* graphics and putting my name on them. Soon after, I learned how to make my own graphics and retired that practice.

We exchanged contact information, and he gave me an open invitation to visit him at the NBC40 station in Linwood. I wanted to set it up immediately but needed to talk to Bebe first.

Looking back on that day a quarter century later, it remains one of the most memorable experiences of my life.

High temperature: 38°F **Low temperature:** 29°F
Conditions: Cold, with light snow showers and building excitement

Today, a weak clipper system slid down from the northwest, bringing just enough cold air and moisture to surprise us with flurries. It wasn't a blizzard, but it didn't need to be. Sometimes the lightest snowfall can spark the biggest dreams. Just like weather, moments that seem small at first can shift the course of your whole life—if you're paying attention.

—Nick's weather journal

Chapter Five

GROUNDHOG DAY

OK, campers, rise and shine, and don't forget your booties
'cause it's cold out there . . . it's cold out there every day.
—*Groundhog Day* (the movie)

Every February 2, without fail, the same routine played out like clockwork. School couldn't end fast enough. I'd all but leap off the bus, my heart thudding with anticipation for the warm fire, the smell of takeout Chinese food, and two hours of laughter wrapped in thick blankets beside Bebe. It wasn't just any night—it was Groundhog Day.

And not just the holiday. I mean the movie. If you're a weather nerd like me, *Groundhog Day* is practically sacred. A weatherman stuck in a time loop? Come on, it was practically written for me. I could recite every line like it was scripture. Bebe and I made it our tradition from the moment I first saw it in the late nineties. I didn't know then how much I'd come to cling to those rituals.

This year, though, something felt . . . off.

I burst through the front door, breathless, cheeks pink from the cold. "Bebe! It's almost time!" I called as I threw my bag down.

She didn't answer. Instead, she sat frozen on the couch, eyes glazed over, *The Maury Povich Show* shouting in the background.

"Bebe?" I stepped closer. "It's movie night! *Groundhog Day*, remember?"

She blinked at me, brows knitted. "What movie?"

I stood still, the air leaving my lungs. My voice faltered. "*Groundhog Day*," I said, trying to laugh, trying to brush off the sudden weight in my chest. "Our movie."

A pause. Then: "Ohhh right. I'm sorry, sweetheart. It's been a long day." Her smile flickered like a candle in a breeze. "But I forgot to grab it. We'll have to go to Blockbuster."

The movie didn't matter anymore. That moment did. My chest tightened. She was forgetting things more often now—little things, then bigger ones. But *this*?

Still, I nodded. "Let's go."

We bundled up, stepping into the frigid wind, the cold biting at our cheeks. The 501 bus creaked to a stop at the corner, and we climbed aboard, her gloved hand gripping mine tightly. The ride across Brigantine was silent except for the hum of the heater and the occasional squeak of windshield wipers against frost.

Blockbuster was packed—of course it was. The blue-and-yellow aisles buzzed with people hunting for something to escape into. I darted through the shelves, fingers brushing over plastic cases. Nothing. No Bill Murray. No Punxsutawney Phil.

Bebe went to the counter. "Excuse me, do you have *Groundhog Day*?"

"Sorry, ma'am. Both copies are checked out," the cashier said with a sympathetic shrug.

I didn't cry over movies. But right then, I felt tears stinging my eyes. Not because the movie was gone—but because, for a moment, so was she.

We opened the door, walked out, and pulled our hoods tight. That's when we heard the thump on the glass.

The cashier waved us down, her voice muffled by the thick glass. "Wait! I found one! It was returned this morning and shelved wrong!"

My heart leapt. I turned to Bebe, who lit up with a smile—the first real one I'd seen all day. For a moment, she looked like the old Bebe again. The one who used to sing Sinatra off-key while microwaving egg rolls. The one who'd quiz me on state capitals while we waited for our takeout—General Tso's chicken, always—with extra fortune cookies. The one who could make even the gloomiest night feel like home.

We skipped the bus and flagged a cab. She leaned into me, the long-lost DVD tucked safely in her bag, and something gentle flickered between us—something like hope. We picked up our usual order, just like old times, and by the time the credits rolled that night, our little tradition had been restored for another year.

I knew these moments couldn't last forever.

But that night, they did.

High temperature: 54°F **Low temperature:** 37°F
Conditions: Overcast with light wind

Today's skies were layered with stratus clouds—thick, gray, and heavy with moisture. They blanketed everything in a dull light, like the world was stuck in a loop of sameness. It reminded me of how routines, like weather patterns, can bring us comfort... until they change. I was reminded today that even the strongest traditions, like our annual *Groundhog Day* movie night, can be disrupted by the slow creep of change we don't always notice until it's too late—like warm air slowly sneaking above a cold front.

But sometimes, even when the forecast seems uncertain, you get a break in the clouds—a reminder that not all is lost. Our tradition was almost broken, but a forgotten movie on a misplaced shelf brought it back to life, if only for one more year.

Weather teaches you to pay attention to the little shifts. Life does too.

—Nick's weather journal

Chapter Six

A FORK IN THE FORECAST

Today is gonna be a GREAT day, Brigantine. We've got sunshine as far as the eye can see. It will be a bit chilly, but we will warm up by the end of the week. Make sure you're wearing layers until then.

—Nick's BRIGANTINE NEWS NETWORK broadcast

I used to spend hours watching The Weather Channel and other local media, observing all the different forecasters do their thing. Most normal kids watch cartoons on the weekend. Me? Nope. I had no interest. My eyes were glued to whatever Jim Cantore was doing and saying.

All of my friends—both of them—thought I was crazy. I practiced weather forecasting like other kids practiced sports. In the shower, I would pretend to be forecasting in front of a green screen. Alone in my bedroom, I used my hairbrush as a microphone and stood in front of the mirror doing "broadcasts."

Even when I was around my friends, I was thinking about the weather.

I told them to look up at the sky: "That cloud formed because there are wind currents going in different directions!" I was a tried-and-true weather geek.

One night, while I was up in my room watching *The Simpsons* as I did every night before dinner, I heard Bebe yell up to me: "Nicky, get down here now!"

I was a bit concerned. I thought something was wrong, so I rushed down two flights of stairs into the kitchen to make sure she was OK.

"Bebe, what is it? Are you alright?" I asked.

"Oh, yeah, I'm fine, but I just saw a commercial for something called Kidcaster. Kathy Orr is going to be at the mall this weekend. We should go," she explained.

Kidcaster? What the heck is that? I thought. I figured I'd turn on the 6 PM news to CBS3 that night and see if Kathy talked about it. Sure enough, at the end of her weather segment, she explained she was going to the local malls to hold auditions to find one lucky kid who had what it took to do the weather live with her in Philadelphia. I turned to my grandmother and screamed with excitement: "Bebe!!!! We need to go. Can we go? Please, please, please!!!"

"Of course we can, Nicky. I'm the one that told YOU about it, after all."

She did have a valid point there.

The next day, I couldn't wait to get to the studio to tell Ms. Kaufman! So many exciting things had happened recently. I had the connection with Dan Skeldon, I had a nickname, I was learning more about weather every single day, and now I'd maybe have a chance to check out what it's like to broadcast the weather in Philadelphia? Crazy! A dream come true for a weather weenie.

That weekend came around. Bebe and I jumped on the 553 bus from Atlantic City to the Hamilton Mall and set out on yet another adventure. This time the adventure was all about me and my love of weather.

We got inside the mall, followed the signage for the competition, and found ourselves at the back of a line that must have been 150 kids deep. Off in the distance, we saw a giant map, tons of lights, a camera, and several workers in blue CBS3 polos.

I looked at the line and got nervous because I realized this same thing was going on all over the area. I think Kathy said earlier in the week she was going to be at nine local malls. That is *a lot* of kids. Could I beat them all? What are the chances that another kid does the weather every day at their school like me?

As we got closer to the front of the line, I observed what each and every kid was doing. The same thing. That was it. Every single kid who stood in front of the camera did exactly the same thing. There was a script mounted underneath the camera to read. I immediately knew what I had to do in order to give myself the best chance of winning this competition—don't do that.

Having looked at the weather models earlier in the day, I knew there was a chance of a storm within a few days. I started to formulate a story in my mind and decided that was how I was going to stand out to Kathy.

We got closer and closer. I finally saw Kathy pop out from behind the map and greet the kid in front of me with a gigantic smile. I was next up.

Someone who was probably a producer stepped up and told me to walk to the line of red tape about ten feet ahead of me and listen for instructions. There she was! Kathy Orr in all her glory. Beautiful, radiant, and glowing. She looked just like she did on TV.

"Hi! I'm Kathy. Thanks so much for coming! Look at the camera, and when we give you the signal, read what's on the paper, then walk off to the side. OK?" she told me.

3 . . . 2 . . . 1 . . . go!

"Hey, South Jersey, I'm Nor'Easter Nick, and boy, do I have good news for you if you like stormy weather. We've got low pressure coming up from the south by Wednesday, which could bring a couple inches of snow our way depending on the track. Today we are in the fifties, but a cooldown is on the way by tomorrow as a front slides through. We'll have more on that coming up tonight at eleven. Back to you, Kathy."

The producer and those behind the camera scratched their heads. One even went to double-check the script. Kathy walked over to me with a confused look on her face.

"Ummm, wow! Did you do all of that from memory?"

"I sure did! I do this every day at school, so I've had a lot of practice. Thanks for doing this! I had fun. Hope to see you again," I said as I looked for Bebe, intending to leave and carry on with the day.

I absolutely killed that, I thought to myself through the rest of the day.

"Bebe, did you see it? How did I do?"

"You were amazing, Nicky. There's no way anyone else here will beat you."

A week or so went by without any word from CBS3. I knew they were going to other malls, but I was worried that I was either not chosen or that they forgot about me. One day after school, the phone rang, and it was Kathy Orr herself! She asked to speak with me.

"Hello?" I said.

"Hi, Nicky! It's Kathy Orr from CBS3. Listen, you did such a great job at the mall we thought we'd invite you to come to our studio this Friday to do the weather with me. How's that sound?"

"Oh my God! Really?! Are you serious? Yes! Absolutely. Count me in!" I replied enthusiastically.

"Great! Can you put your grandmother back on the phone, please, so we can work out the details?" she asked.

Whoa! This was a huge moment for me. *I'm gonna be famous!* I thought. I handed the phone back to Bebe so everything could be finalized, and I immediately pulled out my bus schedules to figure out when we'd have to leave to get there on time.

The conversation between Bebe and Kathy Orr lasted another few minutes, and then everything went silent. I was in the living room trying to be silently nosy.

"Alright, Nicky, looks like you'll be doing the 6 PM news with Kathy on Friday. I'll have to sign you out of school early for us to get there on time."

Friday couldn't come soon enough. I figured if we left Brigantine by 2 PM, we could get to Philadelphia and be there with about an hour to spare.

It was hard to contain my excitement for the next couple of days. I was beaming with happiness and in such a good mood. I told every teacher and all of my friends what I was going to do and made sure they knew to watch. After all, it was my BIG moment.

The day came. I rushed to school to make sure I got all of my work completed early since I needed to be signed out. I finished my broadcast by saying: "Don't forget to watch CBS news tonight at six. I'll see you then!"

Lunchtime rolled around, and I was sitting in Mr. D's office helping him with a few things when the phone rang. It was the main office looking for me. Bebe was there to pick me up.

I never ate in the lunchroom like normal kids because I enjoyed having conversations with Mr. D. Anyone who needed me or was looking for me always knew where to find me. I was either in his office or in the TV studio with Ms. Kaufman.

I quickly gathered all my stuff and beelined to the main office to meet Bebe. You could see her radiance from way down the hall. She always had her hair meticulously done, and, of course, she was dressed in her fur coat.

"Ready to go? Figured I'd come early so we could get a bite to eat in Atlantic City before we get on the bus," she said.

"Yup! Let's go. Bernie is driving the earlier bus, so I can tell him where I'm going!" I replied.

Bernie was one of the bus drivers I'd made friends with since the car accident. I was always looking to get on his bus and talk about the world.

We grabbed lunch at a small diner a block over from the bus terminal, walked to our gate, and waited for the 551 to pull up. Within ninety minutes, the lights of the city came into focus as we approached the Ben Franklin Bridge.

The bus station in Philly was a few blocks from the CBS3 studio. We walked down Market, right into the waiting room of the station, and I introduced myself to the receptionist.

"Hi! I'm Nick Pittman, and I'm here to meet with Kathy Orr—"

Before I could finish, Kathy burst through the door and greeted me.

"Hi, Nicky, I've been looking forward to seeing you all day. This must be your grandmother, Charlotte! Great. Thanks so much for coming. Follow me this way."

I had never seen a building so grand in my life. I was used to our small TV studio, not the grandeur of big-market television. There was glass everywhere. There were computers, lights, and cameras every ten feet, it seemed. I looked around in awe. I was absolutely amazed at what I saw. Everything about this was incredible.

Kathy and Bebe looked back at me every so often and chuckled. They knew I was in heaven.

We got to the end of the long hallway, which was dotted with portraits of current and former anchors on both sides of the wall, and came to a stop at two, what looked like at that age, hundred-foot doors with a bright-red "on-air" sign atop.

In an almost whisper, Kathy said to us, "Be real quiet. Tom is wrapping up his forecast. He will get cranky if he's disturbed. Should only be a few minutes."

"Tom? As in *the* Tom Lamaine that I grew up watching every morning?" I asked.

"Yes, that Tom," she said.

A few moments went by, the on-air sign went dark, and we were allowed to enter the studio. Everything was so bright, shiny, new, and official. We walked over to the anchor desk, and I was introduced to a man named Larry Mendte. He was extremely welcoming and gave me some pointers. Funny thing is—I'd end up actually working with Larry almost twenty years later.

Kathy brought me to the weather center and started looking at the models to formulate her forecast that night.

"This is where we put the graphics together. The model computer is right there and feeds into the graphics computer. We then put the show together using all this information and build a story to tell," she said as she pointed to every piece of equipment.

"We are going to be on at the top of the C block. At six fifteen, we will be live. Let's figure out what you're going to say so you're prepared. I'm going to introduce you and stand off to the side, but I'll come in if you need my help." News shows are stacked and organized into different "blocks" of time. Weather is generally in the A and C block.

It was at that very moment it all clicked. I was confident that this was what I wanted to do for the rest of my life. I'd always known I wanted to work in weather. Though my Jewish grandmother wanted me to become a "docta or lawya," I had other ambitions. Broadcast was where I was meant to be.

For the next half hour, I went over the graphics, rehearsed what I was going to say over and over again, and waited for my big debut. I was nervous beyond belief, but somehow I had a sense of calm come over me because I knew what this moment meant for me and my school. I was there representing Brigantine, and things from that moment would be different.

My first appearance on the news came in the A block. I wasn't speaking, but I was in the background as Kathy did her first weather hit. She teased that she had a special guest in the studio. I knew it was getting closer, and the butterflies in my stomach became a little more noticeable.

It was two minutes until we were live. Kathy walked me over to the green screen, looked at me, and said: "You got this! Just breathe."

3 . . . 2 . . . 1 . . . the red light on top of the camera went solid. We were on.

"We've got a special guest in the studio tonight all the way from Brigantine. Meet Nick Pittman! He goes by 'Nor'Easter Nick' and does the weather every day for his school's TV program. Nick is this year's winner of our Kidcaster competition, and he's got tonight's forecast for you. Take it away, Nick!"

I wasn't used to standing in front of such a large green screen. I felt like my movements were a bit awkward at times, but I made it through the segment very confidently. It was really cool using real weather technology and not a PowerPoint presentation controlled by a classmate behind the computer.

"And that's the weather in your backyard. Kathy will have more at eleven. Back to you, Larry!" I said as I wrapped up the seven-day forecast.

There were loud claps from all corners of the studio. I guess that was a sign that I did a good job.

"Well, Kathy, I think you've got some competition," Larry said before heading into the commercial break.

I walked back over to the weather center, and Kathy had a huge, happy grin on her face.

"I think that was the best performance I've ever seen! You really have a future in this industry."

Those words meant the world to me. To have the approval of someone I looked up to was incredible in every way. Bebe walked over to me, gave me a hug, and told me, "Well done."

Kathy stuck around for a bit after the news wrapped, just to get to know me better. We talked for a solid twenty minutes—easy conversation, the kind that makes time disappear—until Bebe gently reminded us that we had a long trip ahead. We had to hit the road if we wanted to make it back to Brigantine before 10 PM.

I wished we could've stayed longer. Still, even in that short window, it was one of the most memorable experiences of my life.

We exchanged contact info and promised to stay in touch. I would end up inviting Kathy to my school a couple of months after meeting her.

The next day at school was like a homecoming. Everyone noticed me. Everyone had watched. Everyone had a bigger interest in the weather, it seemed. That experience, to this day, I believe, changed the trajectory of my career. It solidified my choice to get into broadcast weather.

High temperature: 54°F **Low temperature:** 39°F
Conditions: Overcast skies with a coastal breeze and low pressure building offshore

Today, a low-pressure system just off the coast reminded me how energy gathers quietly before a storm really begins to spin. It's like life—sometimes, your biggest breakthroughs start with a single chance. One green screen, one moment of courage, and suddenly the entire forecast of your future shifts.

—Nick's weather journal

Chapter Seven

STORM SIGNALS

A BIG change is coming our way this week. High pressure moves out, a series of low pressure systems will be moving in, which will make things much more challenging going forward into the next ten days.

—Kathy Orr, CBS3 broadcast

My grandmother was one of the sharpest people I knew. She didn't have a college education but growing up on the streets of South Philly, she had a doctorate in life. She started her first business at just twenty-one. She got involved in the tavern industry, which was ironic, because she never drank a day in her life. Her passion for business expanded far beyond bars into real estate investing and several one-off ventures. I was always in awe watching her negotiate with some of the shrewdest businessmen out there. She was brilliant and always came out on top with the best end of the deal. She was a very studious person who was always reading books or catching up on the latest info in popular magazines.

Bebe was someone who would quiz me before I had a big test and would not accept anything less than an A for my grade. Sure, I felt pressure to keep her happy and proud, but I knew she always had my best interests at heart, so I always worked as hard as possible to impress her. She taught me algebra years before I had it in school.

This is why it was extremely distressing and saddening to see her mind start to slip over time. It wasn't very noticeable at first, but having spent every waking moment of my childhood with her, I picked up on it. She was starting to forget some basic things like people's names and leaving the stove on after cooking. I hadn't really known how old she was in the moment but after her death I'd find out she was in her early eighties, even though she told everyone—and even passed for—sixties.

Things went into overdrive after she had a bad slip and fall on one of our train adventures. I blame myself for that. I had convinced her to let me stay home from school that day because I wanted to see the new train NJT just brought down to Atlantic City for the teachers' convention. If I didn't press the issue, we would have stayed home, and she wouldn't have fallen.

Once the gate was opened and we were allowed out on the platform, we walked toward the train to board. A man who was walking his German shepherd wasn't paying attention to his surroundings and didn't notice the dog rush in front of Bebe's legs. She was thrown off-balance, and she fell backward toward the train and onto her right hip. She screamed out in agony and several police officers who were sitting inside the station came running out to tend to her.

Within about twenty minutes, the train was heading off to Philly, and we were in the back of an ambulance being rushed to AtlantiCare's emergency room to get her evaluated. I've always had a fear of hospitals so my anxiety was through the roof, plus it was obviously weighing on me that I was the cause of her being in pain.

It took about an hour for the nurses to bring her back for X-rays and then another hour after that for the doctor to come out with a diagnosis.

"Ms. Pittman, unfortunately it looks like you fractured your hip, and we will have to perform replacement surgery," he said.

My heart sank. I kept beating myself up over the whole incident.

"I don't care what you need to do, just stop this pain," she cried out.

Eventually the hospital called my mother—something I was dreading. She needed to be made aware of what was going on because Bebe was going to be out of commission for a while, it seemed.

Two days later, the surgery was completed and it was a success. Almost immediately things seemed very off with Bebe. She was very confused, didn't know what happened, and started calling me by other names. I thought it was just a result of the anesthesia and meds she was on, so I didn't think much of it.

We got her settled back home and came up with a routine to help her recover. I took on a lot more responsibility around the house to make sure everything that needed to get done did. I learned how to cook, paid the bills, and spent time cleaning. It was on me to keep household things moving along and take care of Bebe. I was the man of the house after all.

It was a good four months before she was back on her feet, but she got there, slowly but surely. By that summer she was ready to get out of the house, which meant back to buses and trains. I was happy about that.

Something that really concerned me, however, was the fact that she never seemed to snap out of the confusion that set in after her hip replacement. Before the surgery she became forgetful, but afterward, she was definitely "out of it" more often than not. She confused me for my mother on a regular basis and talked about going to visit *her* mother, who had been dead for probably thirty years at that point.

I didn't know what to do. I didn't want to tell anyone what was going on because I was afraid of being taken away by the state, or worse yet, being forced to live with my mother. I had to cover up what was going on, and luckily I had the ability to take care of everything so I trudged forward.

Eventually I confided in her best friend, Julie, and told her the gravity of the situation and the circumstances I was going through. She was able to convince Bebe to see a doctor to find out if the surgery had any impact on her cognitive state. It was a touchy subject, because Bebe would become very testy when it was brought up.

We met with the doctor. The news wasn't good. He looked at my grandmother and said, "Ma'am, we looked at all the scans, and in my expert opinion, you're very much seeing the onset of dementia. We have some programs we can get you enrolled in to help, but right now there's not a whole lot medically we can do."

She sat there in silence for a good minute before responding.

"So I'm going crazy? Is that what you're telling me?"

"Not at all, but there may be some genetics that you just can't get away from. I know this is going to be an adjustment, and we are here to help you every step of the way. Please reach out with any questions," he responded as he walked toward the door to give us some privacy.

As a kid I had no clue what dementia was, but I assumed it was not a good thing. I knew life was going to be different from that point forward. I did everything in my power to keep this information under wraps.

High temperature: 61°F **Low temperature:** 42°F
Conditions: Overcast, light drizzle

Today's forecast reminded me of the weight of memory—clouds hung low, just like the fog that seemed to settle over Bebe's mind after her fall. When the drizzle started, it wasn't much—just enough to dampen the streets—but it lingered, quietly soaking everything. That's how dementia crept in. Slow. Subtle. Steady. Just as we can't stop the rain, I couldn't stop what was happening to her. But like the umbrella I carry, love became my shelter. And sometimes . . . that's enough to weather the storm.

—Nick's weather journal

Chapter Eight

FINAL DAYS IN BRIGANTINE

Models are picking up on a storm that could develop by the end of the week. Uncertainty is very high with this one. It's either going to blow up into something big and impact the area in multiple ways or fizzle into nothing. We will have more on that coming up in a bit.

—Tom LaMaine, CBS3 broadcast

Since my grandmother's hip replacement, we did less and less together, and she became more homebound as her mental acuity slipped further with each passing month. By then, I was old enough to travel on my own, so I took full advantage of it, heading out on Fridays or Saturdays. I still wanted to continue riding the train and hanging out with Bob and Jen—after all, it had been my routine for so many years. The same route from Atlantic City to Philadelphia.

I really enjoyed helping out the crews and living my fantasy as a train conductor, so I kept going. It was an easy trip: a simple bus ride on the 501 to the Atlantic City Bus Terminal, followed by a short walk to the train station a couple of blocks away. I would leave around two in the afternoon and return just after nine at night.

Bob and Jen both knew that Bebe had the accident and underwent a hip replacement, but they were unaware of the onset of dementia. That was the real reason I preferred traveling alone by that time. They both loved her, talked nonstop, and genuinely enjoyed her company, but they hadn't seen her in over a year.

I had to constantly come up with new excuses to explain why she wasn't coming around anymore. I wanted them to remember Bebe as she was in her prime, not as she was in her current state.

Bob and I had connected on a personal level because he'd had a rough childhood. He was incredibly intelligent and intuitive. I'll never forget what he said to me one night as I was hopping off the engine in Hammonton: "You have to learn to play the hand you're dealt in life. Once you do, everything will be OK."

At the time, I didn't fully grasp the meaning of those words. It wasn't until years later, during a lightbulb moment, that I realized he was right about so many things we talked about in depth over the years.

It became evident that my grandmother's condition had deteriorated beyond what I could handle when she reported me missing. It was a late winter night, and earlier that day, I had told her I was going to hang out with Bob and Jen and would be back later that evening. I had made that exact trip dozens of times. I ensured she was settled in and comfortable before leaving for Atlantic City.

The day started like any other. I saw Jen standing in front of her train on Track 4, smiling as always.

"Nicky, Bob went up to the engine early. You're welcome to ride up there with him or stay back with me. Your call," she said, turning to help a passenger using a wheelchair onto the train.

I absolutely loved riding up on the engine. To me, it was the coolest experience ever—zooming eighty miles per hour through the pines on a fifty-year-old hunk of steel. Amazing! But I didn't want Jen to feel like I preferred Bob over her, so I tried to balance who I'd hang out with each trip. That day, I decided to sit in the cab car and talk with Jen. She always let me hang out in the actual cab, which was cool because I could sit in the engineer's seat and watch the world go by in reverse.

When we arrived in Philadelphia, the passengers disembarked, and Bob pulled the train up to the end of the platform before walking back through the car to meet Jen and me.

"You guys hungry? Let's get some Micky D's," he said.

Grabbing a late lunch or early dinner was customary. Bebe had been obsessed with Au Bon Pain and couldn't resist grabbing an oatmeal cookie—or two or three. So, in honor of her, I walked over there and did the same after we ordered our hamburgers.

We grabbed our food and returned to the train, awaiting our 6:50 PM departure. Not even two minutes after sitting down, the radio blared from the cab.

"NJPD to NJ Rail 4619. Come in, please. Over."

Bob got up, opened the door, and responded, "This is NJ Rail 4619 responding. Over."

"NJ Rail 4619, have you seen a young man, age twelve, brown hair, brown eyes, goes by the name of Nick, on your train?"

"That's a roger, NJPD. Is there an issue?"

"He has been reported missing by his grandmother."

"I assure you he is not missing. He is here with me and my conductor. Over."

"Can you please have him contact his grandmother? Thank you. Over and out."

Bob quickly turned to me, sensing something was off.

"Is there something you need to tell me?"

Damn it. I had no choice but to let him in on what was going on in my life.

"Ummm . . . yeah. Actually, there's a lot to talk about."

The trip from 30th Street Station in Philly to Atlantic City is ninety minutes. Most of that time was spent explaining the situation. You could see the sadness in Bob's eyes as I shared Bebe's dementia diagnosis. It hit close to home for him, as his mother was going through the same thing—a fact I only learned about that night.

When we pulled into Track 1 in Atlantic City, I began my journey home to face whatever awaited me.

"I'm sorry you have to deal with this. I know it's not easy. But don't forget you can talk to either of us anytime you need to, OK?" Bob said as I exited the train.

"I know. Thank you for that. I'll see you guys next week, I hope."

The entire bus ride back to Brigantine, I couldn't stop freaking out. What state of mind must she be in to call the police and report me as missing?

As soon as I stepped off the bus at the corner of our street, I took off running. My heart dropped at the sight of multiple police cars lined up outside our house, their lights flashing in the misty ocean air.

Bebe was close with nearly everyone on the force, so I scanned the scene for a familiar face—someone who might tell me what was happening. My eyes landed on Lieutenant Durant. I rushed toward him, panic rising in my chest.

"Hey, what's going on? I came as fast as I could. I didn't run away; I wasn't lost. She knew I'd be out all day."

"Nick, it's good to see you. Charlotte is upstairs on the balcony with a knife, yelling about ghosts trying to attack her," he said.

Oh no. This wasn't good. Everything I had done to cover up her condition over the past year was about to unravel.

"Oh my God. OK, let me go in and see what I can do," I told Lieutenant Durant.

I entered through the garage and climbed the three flights of stairs to my grandmother.

"Bebe, it's me. Are you OK?"

"I don't know who you are. Get out of my house. I don't want you here," she screamed.

There was no way I could conjure up the ability to hold back my tears. Watching her condition worsen so rapidly was heartbreaking. She honestly didn't recognize me, and that hurt deeply, given the close relationship we'd always had. I was shattered.

"Bebe, calm down. It's Nick. I'm safe. I'm here. You're OK—there are no ghosts," I told her.

After about ten minutes of coaxing, I managed to get her off the balcony and back into her bedroom. In a moment of clarity, she seemed to regain her senses.

"Oh, Nicky, where were you? I'm so sorry. I thought you ran away. Please don't ever scare me like that again, OK?" she said, pulling me into a hug.

That night, I did something I had hoped to avoid—I called my mother and laid everything out. I told her what had happened and that something needed to be done because I could no longer care for Bebe on my own.

We agreed she would come down the next day. It was clear that Bebe would have to sell the house, move into a care facility, and that my days in Brigantine were numbered.

High temperature: 46°F **Low temperature:** 33°F
Conditions: Overcast with occasional breaks of sun

Today, I watched the sun try to push through a thick layer of gray clouds. It made a few valiant efforts—brief moments of warmth and clarity—but each time, the clouds swallowed it back up. It reminded me of the day everything changed with Bebe. One minute, she was herself, the next, lost in the fog. Dementia is like that—brief bursts of sunshine that make you hope, followed by long stretches of shadow. Weather can't be controlled, but we can prepare for it. And in life, sometimes the best we can do is find the strength to keep walking through the overcast.

—Nick's weather journal

Chapter Nine

HEAT WAVES & HARD TIMES

It's going to be another scorcher out there, everyone! We're looking at temperatures reaching up to 92°F with the heat index making it feel closer to 100°F thanks to the high humidity. If you're headed to the beach, don't forget your sunscreen: The UV index is high . . .

—Dan Skeldon, WMGM-TV 40

The New Jersey transit bus stopped near a Wawa convenience store and gas station. From there it was a ten-minute walk to my mother's apartment building in Hammonton, New Jersey. My new home.

The dreaded day had come: The grandmother who raised me was moved to assisted living, and at thirteen years old, I was going to live with parents who were strangers.

I went from a three-story house on the bay off the Atlantic Ocean to a brick apartment building that felt like it was in the middle of nowhere. The town of Hammonton was located directly between Philadelphia and

Atlantic City. It wasn't that far geographically, but it felt like a different planet. There was no water in sight, and it was a shock to my system.

I dragged my heavy suitcase up the stairs of the apartment building, the entrance foyer and halls stifling in the July heat. Outside my parents' unit, I stood for a second, wiping perspiration from my face with the edge of my T-shirt. I knocked. There was no answer. I knocked again, my heart starting to pound with anxiety. I hadn't seen my mother in years.

The door swung open.

"Nick?" my mother said. It was as if I'd shown up unannounced, even though my return had been the subject of weeks' worth of back-and-forth on the phone. Granted, most of that had been with my father.

My parents were an odd couple. They met through my grandmother. When she bought her first house in Brigantine, my father's family lived across the street. At the time, my mother was still living there, even though she was in her mid-twenties. My father, just twenty at the time, was the neighborhood kid who helped Bebe out around the house. And he and my mother hooked up. They'd been together ever since, though they never got married.

My father was healthier emotionally than my mother, but physically he had problems. He was hit by a car as a child and dragged for a mile, leaving him with an arm deformity and blindness in one eye. I guess the two of them compensated for each other's weaknesses in some way. It's hard to make sense of their union otherwise.

I wished he'd been the one to greet me, but it was my mother. She was forty-five years old, petite, with long reddish-brown hair and dark eyes. She was dressed in skinny jeans and a low-cut shirt. She might have been pretty, but her internal ugliness came through. I was a sensitive kid, and her aura was deeply negative.

"Who cut your hair like that?" she said.

My hand instinctively flew up to touch the back of my neck. Before I could answer, she said, "You look like a fag."

The comment felt like a physical blow. I hadn't even stepped into my new home, and she cut right to my deepest insecurity. I knew by then that I didn't like girls. It wasn't something I'd ever discussed with anyone, not even Bebe. I think on some level Bebe knew, and I never doubted that she accepted me completely for who I was. But clearly, that would not be my experience in my new home. I got the message loud and clear: Keep your guard up.

"We've got a full house here," she said. "Baldy is staying on the sofa."

I didn't know who she was talking about, but I would soon learn that my father's brother, Peter, was staying at the apartment too. Everyone called him "Baldy" due to his premature hair loss. My brother Matt was in and out. He would often couch surf at his friends' homes.

"Put your things in the bedroom," my mother said, pointing vaguely to the back of the apartment. I didn't know which room was my bedroom, so I dutifully dragged my suitcase around looking for it. There were only two bedrooms, and both were clearly occupied, with clothes strewn about everywhere. I did not want to reengage my mother, but I needed to ask.

"Which one is mine?" I said, finding her in the kitchen smoking. It was a tiny room with dishes piled in the sink. The view out the window was of a parking lot. It all felt claustrophobic, and I began to perspire more than I had dragging my suitcase across town.

"*Yours?* God, you're spoiled." With a sigh, she gestured for me to follow her back to one of the cluttered rooms. "You'll share this one with me. There's room on the floor."

The thought of having to close my eyes every night next to this woman was unthinkable. I felt utterly trapped. It took everything in me not to cry. How was I going to get through the next several years until I could finally break away for college?

Mercifully, she left me alone to unpack. I sat on the floor next to my suitcase, trying not to hyperventilate. I couldn't take out my things. It would make it too real. If I kept them packed, I knew I could leave at any time. I could pretend I was just visiting.

But I needed one thing: I unzipped the bag and reached inside one of the interior pouches and pulled out my IBM laptop. It was like a pile of bricks in my suitcase, but it was my lifeline. Bebe gave it to me for Christmas a few years earlier so I could have access to weather data.

For the past few days I'd been tracking the National Weather Service's data that suggested a rare type of thunderstorm, called a "derecho," was forming over our area. It was categorized by widespread and sustained winds with sixty-mile-an-hour gusts and a band of rapidly moving showers.

Logging on to my computer, I had the sinking realization that my mother might not have internet access. Even if she did, I'd have to ask her for the password. And I wouldn't go out of my way to interact with my mother. Not ever.

I reached deeper into the suitcase, underneath my clothes, and pulled out a composition notebook. It was my latest weather journal. For the past few years, ever since I started the TV club at school, I'd been keeping a daily record of my forecasts. Weather was an ephemeral thing, so writing it all down was a way to make my work tangible. Something I could look at on a "rainy day."

That day, despite the sunshine, certainly counted as one of them. Every day I spent under that roof would be rainy. And I had no idea how I was going to weather it.

High temperature: 94°F **Low temperature:** 75°F
Conditions: Oppressively humid, no breeze

A strong ridge of high pressure has parked itself overhead, trapping heat and humidity near the surface. There's no movement—no relief. When the atmosphere stagnates, it builds pressure until something has to give. Emotionally, it's not so different. Today reminded me that sometimes the most uncomfortable places teach you how to forecast your own strength.

—Nick's weather journal

Chapter Ten

GROWING PAINS & WEATHER GAMES

Moving in with my family was one of the most difficult transitions I've ever faced. Sure, I no longer had the stress of taking care of my grandmother, but a whole array of new challenges entered my life. Growing up, I had access to anything I wanted. I wouldn't call it "spoiled," because my grandmother always instilled in me that hard work is essential for success, but I was comfortable—I never lacked for anything.

My mother never held a job—not because she couldn't, but because she chose not to. My father, on the other hand, did his best to support us, limited by a disability from an accident years prior. My uncle chipped in when he could, but money was always tight. It was a complete change from where things were prior to moving in with them as my grandmother was self-sufficient. I wanted to do my part, so I landed my first job at a little collectibles shop about twenty minutes from Brigantine—though it took a bit longer coming from Hammonton. Every weekend, I'd spend over an hour riding the train and bus to get there. I never minded. Public transit was my little escape, my place of peace. I made about $150 a week, and $100 of that went to my parents. I went from living with my grandmother in a three-story beachfront home to sleeping on the floor in my mother's bedroom, sharing a small condo in Hammonton with four other people. To say it was a culture shock is putting it mildly. Eventually, the commute to the collectibles store became too expensive, so I started looking for a job closer to home.

I submitted dozens of applications to local retailers but didn't hear back. Taking matters into my own hands, I bought a white dress shirt, a tie, and a pair of black pants. If no opportunities were coming to me, I'd go to them. I walked into ShopRite, the local grocery store, and asked to speak to the manager. Dave, a kind man who bore an uncanny resemblance to George W. Bush, hired me on the spot after I told him I'd do anything to get in the door. A week later, I started as a cashier.

My years at ShopRite taught me invaluable lessons. I made friends and developed my social skills. Despite my experience in front of a camera, I was still somewhat shy. I always wore a shirt and tie instead of the company-issued smock, which made me stand out. Some coworkers disliked me for it, perceiving me as trying to act above my station. My grandmother's advice to "dress for the job you want, not the job you have" has stayed with me to this day.

Within a couple of years, I worked my way up to higher positions in the store and ultimately became a manager by the time I was eighteen.

Taking care of my grandmother had been a significant challenge, but the even bigger test came when life threw a perfect storm of difficulties at me. I nearly broke under the pressure. It felt like I was drowning, and every time I managed to surface for air, something would pull me back under.

I've never had a good relationship with my mother. I struggled to forgive her for giving me up as a child and couldn't understand her bond with my younger brother. They were best friends, and he could do no wrong in her eyes, while I was treated like an outcast. He never worked or contributed, spending weekends drinking and getting high with his friends. I had a chip on my shoulder because of it. I think I was also jaded because I'd think back on the great times we had as kids and it was very upsetting to watch him throw away his life. Sure we lived separately but my mother would on occasion drop him off at my grandmother's to stay the weekend and we made some of the most lasting memories on adventures up and down the Jersey Shore. I missed that. I missed who he was. I hated who he had become. I'd be lying if I said it didn't take some sort of toll on me no matter how much I tried to block it out.

The mental abuse at home was unbearable. I was constantly ridiculed for what I wore, called derogatory names, and blamed for everything that went wrong. There were nights I went to bed hungry because dinner wasn't saved for me after a late shift at work. These small, hurtful acts left lasting scars.

School was my sanctuary. I loved every second of it. Arriving early and staying late, I found safety within its walls. Though I started as "the new kid" at Hammonton High School, I quickly made friends, many of whom remain close to this day. The television program, in particular, became my saving grace. The school had just launched a morning announcements program and was holding auditions. With years of camera experience, I saw it as a natural fit.

Meeting Mr. Josey, the teacher overseeing the program, was life-changing. He hired me on the spot and became a pivotal mentor throughout high school. I spent countless hours in the TV studio, often eating lunch there instead of the cafeteria. Mr. Josey and Mr. Joseph, another teacher who deeply impacted my life, provided guidance and support during some of my darkest times.

While navigating these challenges, I was also grappling with my sexuality. I knew from a young age that I was different, but I forced myself to like girls and even dated a few in high school. Admitting I was gay, even to myself, was a struggle. After high school, I began attending church regularly, hoping to be "cured." If a pill could have made me straight, I would have taken it.

At my lowest point, I considered ending my life. One night, after a heated argument at home, I walked to the train tracks, tears streaming down my face. As the train approached, I was flooded with memories of my grandmother. Her disappointment at my giving up was a vivid image that jolted me back to reality. I turned around and ran home. That moment was my wake-up call.

From that night forward, I vowed to use my struggles as fuel for success. I opened up to trusted mentors like Mr. Josey and Mr. Joseph, who offered invaluable advice. Mr. Joseph introduced me to *The Alchemist*, a book that profoundly shaped my perspective. Its message—that the universe conspires to help those who pursue their dreams with determination—became my guiding principle.

High school remains one of the most cherished periods of my life. I thrived in the structured environment and built lasting relationships with teachers who became friends and mentors. Graduation was bittersweet; I was excited for the future but saddened to leave the safety net that had supported me for four years. As I walked out of those double doors for the last time, I knew I had to chart my own course and tackle the world head-on.

High temperature: 61°F **Low temperature:** 42°F
Conditions: Breezy with patchy clouds

Today, a cold front pushed through, bringing sharp wind gusts and clearing skies. It reminded me how pressure—whether atmospheric or personal—can bring clarity. Storms might shake your foundation, but they also reveal your strength. Even in the darkest skies, there's always a break in the clouds.

—Nick's weather journal

Chapter Eleven

SAFE HARBOR

Good morning, Hammonton! We've got some rocky weather up here in Jersey this week, but things will be clear sailin' for the senior trip down in Disney next week. I'll have another update on that before everyone leaves tomorrow!

—Nick's Hammonton High School broadcast

You've come to know by now that my living situation was far less than ideal. Sure, living with Bebe wasn't *the* ideal, as I always longed for that made-for-Hollywood white-picket-fence-type family with the loving parents, siblings, and a dog, but at least there was a loving home to live in where I wasn't subjected to constant mental abuse.

I did everything I could to take my mind off the situation and not be home. My mother was constantly yelling about something and just genuinely unhappy. She took out her anger on anything and everyone around her. I didn't want to be around it. My father would occasionally snap back at her, but he did his best to avoid the drama. He put his nose down and escaped by working at a local gas station.

Things got particularly depressing around the holidays. I've never been a big gift person because I felt guilty having people spend money on me, and then, in reverse, I didn't have disposable income to be able to get anyone anything. Even with that said, it would have been nice to get *something.*

I poured my heart and soul into the holidays, even when I lived in a place I didn't feel quite welcomed in. After all, the holidays were a big deal for my grandmother and me, and some of my best memories are from November to January.

What little money I did have left over, after paying to live on my mother's floor and covering food for myself, I put into buying Christmas decorations. I remember going to Walmart and the local dollar store to find cheap things to throw up just to brighten the mood. I did what I could to feel more comfortable and give myself a mental break—but even after all of that, the anguish continued.

You should feel comfortable in your home, but I never did. I was always looking for things to do and excuses *not* to be home. I worked a lot, hung out with my close group of friends, and spent a lot of time at school.

The school's TV studio quickly became my sanctuary. I'd show up early, stay late, and often spend my lunch breaks there, lost in a world that made sense to me. I'd run through weather segments on the green screen again and again, determined to improve, driven by something deeper than just passion—it was purpose.

Though I've already talked about Mr. Josey and Mr. Joseph, it's impossible to overstate how much they meant to me during that time. After Bebe and I drifted apart, there was a void in my life I didn't know how to fill. But those two stepped in—not with grand gestures, but with consistency, kindness, and conversation. Every lunch period, we'd talk. And for whatever reason, I felt safe enough to open up to them about things I'd never tell anyone else.

Mr. Josey, with his background in Philadelphia television, shared his real-world experience generously. He'd seen life from the inside out—grown up rough, broken ties, and all. I always felt as though there was a strong connection there since he understood what it was like to have to fend for yourself. And Mr. Joseph, with his calm, big-picture wisdom, helped me see that the world wasn't something to fear—it was something to shape. He lived by *The Alchemist*, a book he taught with so much conviction that it still echoes in my life today.

Looking back, I realize those quiet moments—those talks, that space, that encouragement—helped shape who I was becoming. School was always easy. Talking wasn't. But those two made it easier to be myself. And for that, I'll always be grateful.

One day at lunch we started talking about the senior trip that was coming up after the new year. Everyone was over the moon excited about it. Everyone but me.

"So, Nick, are you looking forward to the trip? I bet I can go on more roller coasters than you and not barf!" Mr. Joseph said laughing.

I kept my glance toward the floor. "I wish I could go. We don't have money like that, and anything I make from ShopRite goes right to my parents. I'm not gonna be able to go."

He put his hand on my shoulder, was silent for a moment, but then finally uttered, "It's OK. I understand. Hey, I have to cut this short; I've got a meeting with Mr. Ramsey. Let's catch up tomorrow morning, OK?"

It really sucked that I wouldn't be able to go. Apparently, from everything I'd heard, this trip was a really big deal, and the amount of fun everyone had—both students and teachers—was next level. Major FOMO (fear of missing out) was settling in.

The next day rolled around. I wasn't my chipper self because payments for the trip were due to the office to solidify airfare and hotel accommodations. Obviously, knowing I wasn't going and how I was going to explain it to my friends was weighing on me.

I saw Mr. Joseph in the corner of my eye standing out in the hallway. He was trying to get my attention, or at least I thought he was. I looked up and saw him motioning for me to come out and meet him.

"Here you go. Take this down to the office," he said as he handed me a plain white envelope.

"Aye aye, Captain; I'll be right back." I took it and walked down the hall, which was teeming with kids trying to get to their homeroom before the bell rang.

I didn't think anything of it. I was asked to bring things to the office every day since all the teachers knew I was going to get the task done and not get "lost." I was very curious as to what this envelope was. It wasn't sealed, so I knew it wasn't top secret or anything. So I took a peek.

I saw a note that had my name on it. I felt like I had the green light to pry further. I ducked into the bathroom just before the office and unfolded the note. It read:

"Nick—I know it must be hard to want things and not have the ability to have them. You are a good kid and you are going places. Take this. I am covering the cost of your trip. Pay it forward. —Gary J."

A check for $1,250 was taped to the bottom of the note.

I broke down crying like I had just won the Mega Millions lottery. No one had ever been that generous to me in my life. This guy took enough interest in me to help me go on the senior trip, and I couldn't have been more grateful.

After bringing the check to the office, I booked it back to the studio. Mr. Joseph was sitting at his desk when I walked in. I walked over, knocked on the door, and asked, "Hey, can I come in?"

"Absolutely," he responded.

I closed the door behind me.

"Mr. Joseph, I . . . I . . . I have no words. Thank you so much. I don't know how long it will take me to repay you. I don't make a whole lot," I said.

"Nick, don't worry about it. How about this? I own a photography business. Come out this weekend—we are shooting a Little League team in Pitman. I'll teach you how to take the pictures, and you can work it off that way. Deal?"

My eyes lit up. "Deal!" I left his desk and found my seat, absolutely blown away by what had just happened.

That weekend rolled around, and I met him in Pitman and spent a good four or five hours shadowing him and his team. I learned a lot, and I grasped the process pretty quickly. I just wondered how many times I'd have to do it to pay off my trip.

"What do you think of this stuff? Do you like it?" he asked at the end of the day.

"I love this. It's really a lot of fun! How many times do you want me to come out?" I asked.

"Oh, that's up to you. Consider yourself paid in full. Now anytime you want to make more money, you can come work for me at twenty-five dollars an hour," he told me.

I was dumbstruck. I can't remember anyone being so nice and generous to me. He really just gifted me my senior trip.

"Mr. Joseph. You don't have to do that. I can pay you back."

"Pay it forward. One day when you are in a position to do so, make a difference in someone else's life," he said as he walked back to his car.

I ended up working for his company for a couple years. It was great side money, especially at that age. I made much more than I did at ShopRite pushing carts. There were times I would call out of work there if he had a job because I knew I'd be more appreciated and would make out better.

I've got a special affinity for teachers because of the impact so many had on my life. From elementary school to high school, I had some of the kindest, most caring teachers that always wanted to see the best for me.

There is a very good chance that I would not be the person I am today if it wasn't for the amazing educators in my life at all levels. They deserve our utmost respect and admiration. What they do is extremely difficult and selfless. Let's face it: They surely aren't doing it for the money.

In everything I do, every action I take, I think about the people who pushed me, and in the back of my mind, I want to continue doing things that will, in some odd way, make them proud, whether they know it's happening or not.

Mr. Joseph and Mr. Josey saved me. I honestly don't know what path I would have gone down if I didn't have them to talk to and guide me. They were some of the most important influences I had in my life at that age. It is because of them that I actually got into television at such a young age.

One afternoon I walked into Mr. Josey's office, and he had a smirk on his face. He was typically hard to read, but on that day I knew he was in a super good mood. "I just emailed you something," he told me.

"What is it?" I was very curious. I thought maybe it was something to do with the upcoming Ten Day Film Challenge we were all prepping for.

I raced to my inbox—it was a link to a job opening at WMGM-TV 40.

"Weekend Meteorologist, must have proficient speaking abilities, forecasting skills, and ability to work nights and weekends," the posting said.

"That's really cool. Maybe one day I'll get my chance to do this. I watched TV40 as a kid with my grandmother. It's got a special place in my heart," I told him.

He looked at me, leaned over his desk, and said, "Maybe that one day is now?"

I looked back at him and laughed. “You don’t . . . I can’t . . . Why would they pick me?”

“Nick, look at that posted next to the clock over there. You guys look at it every day. It’s there for a reason.”

Aside from being our media teacher, Mr. Josey was also one of the school’s basketball coaches, so he had a lot of motivational sports quotes around his classroom. I squinted my eyes and made out: “You miss 100% of the shots you don’t take.” I looked back at him and said, “But, Mr. Joseph, I’m seventeen. I’m just a kid.”

He glared back at me with that grin and said, “And your point is?” and motioned back to the poster by the clock. “You do a really good job every day. You know your stuff and you’re polished. There are kids coming out of college that don’t have a tenth of the talent you do. Put together a demo video, I’ll help you, and send it out. You never know.”

I thought about it long and hard and was silent for a few moments. *Could he be right?* I wondered. After all, he *did* have a couple decades of media experience under his belt. I’d trusted him on everything else to this point, so why not now?

“Alright. I’m in. I’ll start making the demo tomorrow.”

“No. You’re gonna start today. Meet me at 3 PM. I don’t have practice today,” he said.

“OK, OK. Got it. See you then.”

Later that afternoon, I spent time putting a demo show together. I wanted to be able to showcase more than the minute I got every morning on the announcements, so I built a longer show. We had some thunderstorms coming through that day, so it was a prime opportunity to talk about things I never really had a chance to. I even roped my best friend, Josh, into it and convinced him to be the anchor so we could have cross talk.

There was a point when I ran home for a shirt and tie to look more professional. I thought it was worth it. I pulled up radar maps, models, and video of severe weather out to our west. I did an in-depth explanation of how tornadoes formed and added in some of my morning announcement hits to showcase my personality.

I was at the school until about six that night. Mr. Josey was still there with me in his office, grading papers. Once I finalized shooting and putting together all the clips I wanted to use in a storyboard in the editing software, I went to Mr. Josey for his approval.

"Here's what I got. What do you think?"

There was about five minutes of content that he watched. I couldn't really gauge how much he liked it—or didn't like it. So I twiddled my thumbs and waited for him to say something.

"It's too long. You've got good material, but if I'm a news director or GM, my attention is gone after about a minute. We want to put the most impactful stuff right up front. Rearrange and show me tomorrow. OK?"

"Yes, sir. I guess I should pack up and go home anyway. It's dinnertime. I'll see you tomorrow," I said as I grabbed my book bag and headed for the exit.

My parents' apartment building was about a mile from the school. I walked every day, rain, snow, or shine. My mother used to pick up and drop off my brother, but she rarely ever extended that courtesy to me.

We had just had rain the day before, so it was one of those muddy situations.

The next day came around, and I met with Mr. Josey first thing in the morning and made the final edits to the demo reel. He approved of my latest version and told me to burn it to a CD.

"OK . . . soooo . . . now what?" I asked him.

"Now you're going to type up a résumé and a cover letter and send it out in the mail."

He had taught us how to prepare these materials earlier in the year as part of his curriculum. I was so ready to get the ball rolling that I took the time at lunch to get it done. I went to the office after it was completed and asked for a large envelope. I placed the résumé in a report cover inside the oversized envelope with the CD containing the demo reel. After school I rode my bike over to the post office and mailed it. Truthfully, I never expected to hear back. After all, I was just a junior in high school. What would they want with me?

A few days went by and I nearly forgot about it because I really thought it was a *very* long shot given my age and lack of professional experience, until my phone rang. I was driving so I just glanced at the unrecognized number and let it go to voicemail. When I got to my destination and threw the car in park, I fumbled to open my phone so I could listen to the message.

"Nick, it's Dan Skeldon from WMGM-TV 40. I remember you from when you were a kid. Listen, I got your résumé in the mail yesterday and I'm very impressed. I'd love to have you come to the station next week for an in-person demo and interview. OK, give me a call back when you get a chance."

Oh my God. It's happening, I thought. My teachers were right! I had a very strong feeling that I was about to enter the field I had been dreaming about since I was a kid. It was an overwhelming, incredible feeling.

High temperature: 54°F **Low temperature:** 41°F
Conditions: Drizzle, gray skies, muddy fields

Some days feel like walking through mud—one step forward, and you're stuck. Today started clear: Someone believed in me, handed me an envelope full of hope. But by dinner, the kitchen was empty, and so was the feeling.

Still, mud means the ground is changing. One day, I'll be the one handing out sunshine after someone else's storm.

—Nick's weather journal

Chapter Twelve

AUDITION FOR A DREAM

I could hardly believe it when I was offered the chance to interview at NBC40. I kept pinching myself, half-convinced it had to be a dream. It was one of those rare, surreal times when everything you've worked for starts to line up—and in that moment, I remembered something Mr. Josey once said: *"When you give your all—when you chase what you want with everything you've got—the universe takes notice and meets you halfway."*

That idea stuck with me. It echoed what Mr. Joseph and *The Alchemist* had taught us: If you focus your energy on your goals, the universe will conspire in your favor. I've seen it unfold time and time again in my life. When I stopped giving attention to negativity and poured everything into positive action, my whole mindset shifted—and so did my path. Suddenly, what once felt impossible started to feel within reach.

Mr. Joseph would always tell us to visualize what we wanted. *"See it in your mind first,"* he'd say. *"Live there in your thoughts, and one day, it'll be real."* I took that to heart. That NBC40 interview? It was the first major sign that he was right.

So many times I pictured myself on TV. I saw myself in front of the green screen looking at moving maps and talking to an audience. I lived it every day at school, but I felt deep in my bones that I was going to be doing it for *real* one day. I finally had my opportunity, and I was very well aware of the significance of the moment because I was still, quite literally, only a kid. Even if I didn't get the job, the very idea that a TV station would consider me was big enough.

After taking the bus and train to get where I needed for years, I finally had a car to call my own. It wasn't glamorous, but it got me from A to B. I enjoyed riding public transit but being able to drive anywhere I wanted at any time was a game changer. I hopped in the car and made the forty-five minute drive down to Linwood.

I pulled up into a dimly lit parking lot and walked toward a half-rusted gray door without a window. After pushing the buzzer, I waited for someone on the other side to answer.

"Hello, welcome to NBC40 News. How can I help you?" a commanding voice said.

"Hi! I'm Nick Pittman and I have an interview with Dan Skeldon," I said.

"Just a moment. Someone will be right out."

I feel like most normal people would have been nervous at that moment, but for whatever reason I felt completely at ease. I was confident in my abilities and knew that everything I had done and practiced had led me right to that point.

The door swung open. "Nicky! No, wait, I'm sorry, Nick! It's been forever—how the heck are ya?" a friendly Dan Skeldon said as he grabbed my hand and shook it.

"I'm well; it's good to see you. Yeah, it has been a while now, hasn't it?"

"Alright, we are gonna go through this hallway and hang a left. Harvey is waiting for us." Dan motioned to the back of the office.

It was a small, stuffy building, but to me—a weather and TV geek—it may have well been the Taj Mahal. We walked down the hall and knocked on the door of an office where a larger gentleman in his sixties was sitting at his computer, looking down.

"Harvey, Nick is here," Dan said.

Harvey took his glasses and perched them atop his head. "Yes, of course. Dan, Nick, come in." He extended his hand and greeted me. "Have a seat."

Dan started the conversation with an icebreaker recounting the time six years prior when he visited my school to see me do the weather. He really sold me as a hard worker and someone who would be a good fit for the job.

Harvey said, "So Nick, I'm going to be up front with you. I normally wouldn't be having this conversation. You're seventeen. You don't have a college degree and you don't have any real television experience." I immediately began to feel my jaw clench because I thought the meeting was going to go in a not-so-positive direction. "But," he continued, "Dan here seems to be your biggest fan and believes you'd be a great fit. You guys are gonna go back into the studio and make a video. I want to see how you do in our environment. I'm not promising anything, but I'm at least open to the idea."

"Well, sir, thank you. That means a lot to me. I've watched this station since I can remember. It would be an honor to be considered. If I'm given the chance, I promise you won't regret the decision," I told him as I extended my hand.

"Nice meeting you, Nick. Good luck. Perhaps we will talk again soon."

Dan walked me into the studio, and we made our way back toward the weather center. It was an interesting set. I later found out they got the desk and façades from a station in New England that underwent a major renovation. Truth be told, we had better technology in elementary and high school. Most of the cameras on the studio floor were clearly from the nineties. Everything appeared held together with bubble gum and tape, but there was a certain charm about it all that made anyone who walked in overlook the shortcomings.

"We are gonna go over some of the weather models and get a firm understanding of the forecast, then I'll have someone in master control record a couple hits. I'll give you a practice run or two if you need," Dan told me as we sorted through information on his computer.

"Looks like we've got a pretty deep trough on the way, and I think that could spark some snow showers along the clipper that comes through tomorrow. Could even be good for a couple inches," I said back to him.

"You really do know your stuff, huh?"

"I wouldn't be here if I wasn't serious."

"Good point," he replied.

For the next hour we went over the upper air pattern, temperature profile, and positioning of the highs and lows across the country in depth. I felt like I had a pretty solid footing under me and was ready to hit the green screen.

A young lady, Cara, emerged from master control, greeted me, and told me what signals to look for to indicate everything was recording.

"And if you mess up or want to redo something, just stop and let us know," she said as she faded into the dark hallway near the control room.

Alright, it was now or never. This was my shot.

"Good evening, South Jersey! I'm Nor'Easter Nick Pittman and boy do I have good news for you if you're a snow lover. Let's first take a look at Doppler radar. I know it doesn't look like much at the moment, but see this piece of energy over the Upper Peninsula of Michigan? That is going to gain a little traction, and by the time it gets down into the Delaware Valley, could bring us a light dusting of snow. If everything works out *just* the right way, up to a couple inches is possible."

I went on for a few minutes without skipping a beat even one time. I hung up the clicker, walked over to Dan, and said, "How'd I do?"

He looked back at me and immediately said, "Well, I guess you don't need a practice run, do you?"

"I think I've had plenty of practice lately," I told him, smiling ear to ear.

"So when do you think I'll know?" I asked.

He returned a question: "What are your plans for the last weekend in December?"

"I don't have anything on my agenda. It's Christmas but I don't really have a close family so we don't do much," I told him. "Why do you ask?"

"I'm on vacation starting the twenty-fourth. I know it's a lot to ask, but do you think you'd be able to cover for me?"

"Ummm . . . yes, sure. I mean don't you have to check with Ha—"

"Trust me. You're in," he said. "Once I show Harvey your hit from tonight, believe me, he will be sold. Welcome to the team."

He extended his hand, but I could have hugged the man.

"I'll be in touch with a list of things to do by tomorrow or the next day. You'll want to shadow me for a full day so you're aware of all the procedures. We will talk soon!" he said.

"Dan, I can't thank you enough for the opportunity. I won't let you down," I told him as I turned to walk out of the studio and toward my car.

The whole thing felt surreal. The first thing I did was text Mr. Josey and Mr. Joseph. "Interview went well. I got the job. I start in ten days."

Almost immediately I got a response from both offering me congratulations. I did it. I was a junior in high school, only seventeen, and I had a job for a real-life, honest-to-goodness NBC affiliate. That was the start of what would become a very long and fruitful career.

High temperature: 48°F **Low temperature:** 29°F
Conditions: Mostly sunny with a light breeze

There's something about cold, clear days that make the horizon look sharper—like the world is full of possibility. That's how today felt walking into my first TV station interview. I used to dream about pointing at maps on a green screen, and now here I was, standing in front of one for real. Like a surprise high-pressure system settling in after a string of gloomy lows, the energy shifted. All the practice, all the dreaming—it came together.

Sometimes, life gives you your forecast early. But you've still got to show up and deliver the weather.

—Nick's weather journal

Chapter Thirteen

FORECAST: BRIGHT FUTURE

I wish you all nothing but the best and a future filled with sunshine, blue skies, and high pressure. I am officially handing over the clicker to North Pole Noel. It has been an honor bringing you the weather every day for the last four years and hope you check me out on NBC40 every weekend! Stay classy, Hammonton!

—Final Hammonton broadcast

I was the quintessential nerd through school. With a rough family life, school was very much an escape for me. I was sad to see it all come to an end. I know most of my friends were excited to move on, to go to college and party it up, but that was never the plan for me. I didn't know exactly which direction life would take me.

I had the job at TV40 doing weekend weather, but I also worked full-time for ShopRite and was all but guaranteed a promotion to management—something that was very rare for someone so young.

No, I wasn't doing the traditional four-year college thing. It wasn't that I didn't have the grades; it was because I didn't *want* to go. In fact, I graduated with a 4.0 and was accepted with a full ride to Penn State. It's the dream school for anyone wanting to major in meteorology.

When the time came, however, I couldn't accept. I felt guilty. Bebe was in a nursing home, and I couldn't stomach the idea of leaving her to start my life over a few hundred miles away. She didn't know me as my seventeen-year-old self, but she'd talk about me to me, and that's all that I needed to keep that connection alive. Aside from the dementia, she was healthy, and I thought she had a couple good years left.

I visited her every day and would stay by her bed for a couple hours. It was a big change from where things had been a few years prior, but she was still with us, and that's all that mattered to me. As long as she was coherent enough to speak, even if it was about the past, I still wanted to be around and see her as much as I could.

My plan after graduation was to put my head down, focus on my career, and try to make strides to better myself. I was conflicted. NBC40 wanted to hire me full-time, but ShopRite management promised a much higher salary. Ultimately I chose to go full-time at ShopRite and stay part-time with NBC40, a decision that would later turn out to put me at a great advantage down the road.

The summer of 2010, right after graduation, was one of the most unforgettable times of my life. While I spent a lot of time alone at the school TV studio and talking with my teachers, I did have a tight-knit group of friends—Josh, Denise, Morgan, and Megan. We'd take turns hanging out at one another's houses, where we'd play board games, bake, and watch movies.

Everyone was about to scatter across the country, chasing new beginnings. I was the only one who stayed behind—and while I had my reasons, it didn't make saying goodbye any easier. The late nights, the inside jokes, the feeling that nothing else mattered but that moment—it was all coming to an end. And I knew life was about to change. All of the things I enjoyed for four years were coming to an end. It was time to write a new chapter.

I was particularly melancholy about Josh moving away. We were the closest out of the group and did a lot of things together. He was an only child and I was raised as if I were one. We connected on a different level—it was like we were more than friends; we were family. There was a time when his parents took me in for a little while after a falling-out with my parents. I had nowhere to go and they were there for me.

Throughout the years Josh and I would visit his grandparents at their home in the Pocono Mountains and even go on vacation to their timeshare in Daytona Beach. Even though I felt like I hadn't belonged in my own family, I always felt welcomed in Josh's. We would ride bikes all over Hammonton in the heat of the summer and explore trails in the middle of the woods during other parts of the year. He was the brother I never had. I couldn't help but tear up at the thought of losing all of that, but I managed to come to terms with it and did what I do best—pour all my time and attention into work.

While we don't see each other often, our little group makes it a point to get together a couple times a year. We started a tradition well over a decade ago to meet for pizza at one of our favorite restaurants, Marcello's in downtown Hammonton, during the Mt. Carmel Festival. It's nice to be in everyone's company and reminisce about old times.

Once I was promoted into management with ShopRite, I was sent to the Absecon store—the very store where I had many memories shopping with my grandmother. Many of the employees who worked there when I was a little tyke were still there when I became their front-end manager, which felt like a full-circle moment.

It was extremely intimidating at first, but I found my groove and was able to grow personally and professionally. My bosses treated me well and knew that working in television part-time was important to me. They were flexible and understood if I needed to work on a major storm. In some way, I think working in TV was beneficial to ShopRite because the customers all watched the station, and it improved our community relations.

There were weeks I'd work eighty hours between the two jobs, but I loved every minute of it, and I loved the paychecks that came along with all the hard work. The more I worked, the less I saw my grandmother. I went from seeing her every day of the week to five times a week to a few times a week to, eventually, a few times a month.

Her condition continued to deteriorate. It got to a point where she didn't even know who she was anymore. The nursing home staff would often have to keep her away from the other residents because she'd become violent and throw things. When I would stop and visit, she'd often get nasty with me, because she had no idea who I was.

I'd be lying if I said that it doesn't bother me, even today. I absolutely hate that I stopped seeing her. It eats at me. I've tried for years to justify it. I just didn't want to see her in the condition she was in before the end. I wanted to remember her as the strong, beautiful, sharp woman that raised me. She was a shell of her former self. There were times I'd visit and she'd be nonverbal, just sitting in a wheelchair staring blankly into the void. My heart was ripped to shreds every time I walked into that nursing home. I couldn't bear to see her like that.

One day, while I was working the front end at the grocery store, the chaotic checkout lanes buzzing with customers and carts, I got a call. It was the kind of call you brace for without even realizing it. Deep down, I always knew it would come, but I thought I had more time. Years, maybe. Instead, right there between scanning groceries and managing a line that never seemed to end, I was hit with it, reality, calling in the middle of the noise. "Hello, Mr. Pittman? This is Doctor Giampetti over at the nursing home. Listen, I'm so sorry to have to tell you this, but Charlotte passed away at ten o'clock this morning," the voice on the other end of the phone said.

"Wow. Well, thank you for letting me know, Doctor. I appreciate you calling." I hung up, put my head in my arms, and sat at the podium for a few minutes.

My assistant, Tara, knew something was off immediately. She walked over to me and said, "Why don't you go take a breather outside? I've got this."

"Thank you," is all I could muster.

I walked out to my car and burst into tears. The oddest thing was the fact that I wasn't just crying out of sadness. Don't get me wrong, the whole situation sucked and I was really upset that she was no longer with me, but at the same time I was crying out of relief. She was no longer suffering. She didn't have to fight anymore. She didn't have to live in the past. She didn't have to wonder when someone was going to come visit her.

All the amazing memories from the past came rushing back into my mind. I couldn't help but smile every time I thought of her. In my memory she will live on as I knew her in the 1990s and early 2000s. She was strong. She was vibrant. She was a shark of a businesswoman, and I refuse to remember her any other way.

Still, though, I regret not being there in the very end. That woman gave me every ounce of effort and love she could. I've never been the religious type, but all I can hope is that if there is another life or something that comes after this, she can still see in some way that I've worked so hard to make her proud. She taught me so much, and she was there for me every step of the way when I needed a mother figure most.

I remember being a kid and looking up to her and thinking, *I want to be just like her when I grow up.* I hope that no matter where she is right now, she can be proud of me and what I've accomplished, knowing that what she taught me is the very foundation and bedrock of it all.

Anytime I'm down and need a pick-me-up, I think about her. I think about what she would say or do and I shake it off. She has been gone for well over a decade now, but I can recall the deep conversations we had when I was a child like it was yesterday. She will forever be the most impactful person in my life, and I will never forget anything about her.

Graduation day came around. It's usually a big family affair with everyone's parents, grandparents, and siblings sitting in the stands cheering them on. For me, I had none of that. No parents, no grandparents, no one. My own mother didn't bother to show up for me. My father had an excuse—he was always working; I didn't put any blame on him. He had to do what he could to pay bills and put the little food we did have on the table.

I worked my ass off through high school to graduate among the top in my class. I did it for me, but I also did it to prove a point. Graduation was the first major event that my mother didn't come to; my wedding, several years after, would be the next. Even though we didn't have a good relationship, it still hurt. It hurt because while I was a fiercely independent person even at a young age, it would have been nice to see someone that was blood in my corner.

"And with that I wish the graduating class of 2010 a big congratulations and wish you the very best going forward," our superintendent said in the closing moments of the ceremony. Before I knew it, the sky was eclipsed by hundreds of blue caps.

I walked off the football field and back into the TV studio to close things down for one last time. So many memories in that room. It was all over. I could never go back, but I also didn't *want* to go back because I knew I had an opportunity to chart a new course and start my life over. That day would become the first day of the rest of my life, and I'd never look back even for a moment.

Before leaving for good, I spotted Mr. Joseph standing at the end of the hall looking back at me.

"Nick, what are you still doing here, man? Go! Go have fun. Go start your life!" He patted me on the shoulder.

"I . . . I . . . I just want to really thank you for everything you've done for me. I really needed someone like you in my life, and you were there for me. I'll never be able to repay you for what you did for me. Thank you so much, Mr. Joseph." At that point I started tearing up.

He reached out for a hug and told me, "You're a good kid, Nick. Mark my word, you will do big things. I'll always be a phone call away if you ever need me."

"Thank you; that means lot. I guess it's not goodbye, but I'll see ya later," I told him.

"Yup, that's absolutely right! And I've got some photo jobs coming up over the summer if you're still interested!"

I would end up working for Mr. Joseph's photography company for another couple years.

High temperature: 75°F **Low temperature:** 58°F
Conditions: Clear skies with a soft breeze

Tonight the sky was quiet—no storms, no clouds, just calm. But sometimes, calm can feel heavy too. I've learned that in life, like in weather, the stillest nights can carry the loudest memories. Graduation marked the end of one chapter and the beginning of another, but it also reminded me of everything and everyone I carried with me—including the ones who couldn't be there.

Just like a gentle breeze still holds the scent of a passing storm, our memories hold power long after the moment is gone.

—Nick's weather journal

Chapter Fourteen

TRIAL BY SNOW

Snow will begin falling late tonight around 10 PM. Strong winds are expected to accompany the snowfall at 14–24 mph with gusts up to 35 mph. Tonight, temperatures will drop to the mid-20s. Expecting significant travel delays and road closures.

—Nor'Easter Nick, WMGM-TV 40

"What are you smiling about?" my mother said when I walked into the kitchen. She was dressed in a robe and knockoff UGGs, and her face showed traces of makeup from the night before.

I had been avoiding her as much as possible, sometimes even sleeping at the news station. There was a small cot behind the weather center. The studio had thin walls, and I could hear the traffic on Route 9 all night. I had a tiny space heater and some blankets, and every now and then one of the control room operators would check on me. It wasn't comfortable, but I preferred sleeping in a cold, dark studio than in the same room as my mother. I never knew what version of her I was going to get when I walked in the door.

“Big day at the station,” I said, opening the fridge at home to see if there was, by some miracle, anything to eat. There wasn’t. “I’m doing my first broadcast.”

Today would be my trial by fire—or, I should say, trial by snow. A blizzard was shaping up for our area, and our weather chief, Dan Skeldon, was on vacation. I would be the only one talking our audience through our worst storm in years.

My mother did not look impressed.

“What are they paying you at that place?”

The question felt like a non sequitur. But I gave her an honest answer. She shook her head. “You make twice as much at ShopRite. Why are you wasting your time?”

I turned to her. At this point, her words shouldn’t still have had the power to hurt me, but somehow they did.

“Because . . . this is what I want to do. For my career.”

“Nick,” she said, as if I were still a small child and she had to muster the patience to deal with me, “that is never going to happen.”

I felt like I was going to cry, but I fought back the tears. I wouldn’t give her the satisfaction. Instead, I went straight to the bedroom and closed the door. It wouldn’t do much good since it was her room too. But at least I could buy a few minutes of privacy while I retrieved my weather journal from a shoebox under the bed.

It wasn’t there. I knelt down and reached deeper into the dark space. Nothing. I opened the shades to get more light in the room and saw only empty floor. My heart started pounding.

My mother had found it. There was no doubt in my mind she’d thrown it away.

Tears filled my eyes. I wanted to curl up in a ball right there on the floor. But then I reminded myself: My journal was gone, but I had something just as good—maybe better.

As of that afternoon, I’d have an audience.

I stepped onto the stage set of WMGM-TV 40, New Jersey. Behind me, the green screen was a piece of painted plywood. The news station was physically small. Everything felt kind of held together by duct tape, but it worked for our audience. WMGM-TV 40 was beloved by the people of Southern New Jersey.

Directly in front of me, the tally light on the camera turned red, telling me that we were on the air. A million thoughts raced through my mind—none of them about the weather: I was dressed wrong. My blue jacket and khaki pants were way too big for me. I looked ridiculous.

"You can do this," the news director whispered in my earpiece.

I hoped he was right. Every single day of my childhood had been preparing me for this moment.

The news anchor on-air said, "We've got blizzard warnings up and down the coast for winds to reach over sixty miles per hour and snow totaling over two feet in some areas. For more on that, let's head over to the weather center with our very own Nor'Easter Nick. Nick, over to you."

This was it. I'd been going by the name Nor'Easter Nick ever since Dan Skeldon bestowed it on me in third grade, but never *professionally*. In that moment, it became very real.

I took a deep breath, smiled, and looked at the camera. "I'm Nick Pittman, and a significant winter storm is set to impact New Jersey, bringing heavy snowfall, strong winds, and hazardous travel conditions. This storm is expected to affect the region starting late tonight and continuing through tomorrow evening. Let's take a look at the current conditions and what you can expect over the next twenty-four hours."

All afternoon, I'd been tracking the other news channels. I collected my own data, but we all worked off of the same public information: The National Weather Service released balloons into the atmosphere twice a day. All that data collected by the balloons was free and available, and that's what we plugged into our forecast models. We looked at ten to fifteen different models. Some were calibrated for ten to fifteen days in the future. Others gave us fine detail for one or two days in the future, and those were higher resolution models. So we looked at all that stuff—the models saying this, and the real-time satellites saying that, and radar saying this, and from there, we built our forecasts. The models often showed something different than what was actually happening in real time.

I faced the little red camera light, thinking about the thousands of people watching me. I was barely able to speak and breathe at the same time.

"As you can see on our weather map, the snowstorm is centered over Southern New Jersey, bringing heavy snowfall, gusty winds, and significantly reduced visibility. Right now, we're seeing snowfall rates of about one to two inches per hour, with totals expected to reach twelve to eighteen inches by the time the storm passes."

My breathing was so irregular that my voice crept higher up the register. I didn't know if I'd make it through the broadcast without sounding like a cartoon character. And then it hit me—nearly fifteen years after watching Jim Cantore on TV covering the Blizzard of '96, I thought, *How can I channel my inner Jim?* I imagined his enthusiastic yet controlled demeanor, no matter how extreme the weather. Jim Cantore was always Jim Cantore, rain or shine. He didn't let his circumstances, his environment, shake him.

I could do this. I got my breathing regulated, and my speaking voice followed. By the time I segued into my closing, I sounded professional.

"Snow will continue to fall heavily through the evening and into the night. Expect an additional six to ten inches of snow by morning. Winds will remain strong, with gusts up to thirty-five miles an hour."

I closed with public safety warnings and signed off with: "We'll keep you updated with the latest information throughout the night."

The cameras cut back to the news anchors, and I exhaled.

"Good job," the director called out.

"Thank you," I said. I'd flubbed a few words, but no one seemed to have noticed. I'd gotten through my first live broadcast, and I was officially on the path to following in Jim Cantore's footsteps. In that moment, I felt like I could sprint the rest of the way.

I was wrong.

High temperature: 28°F **Low temperature:** 15°F
Conditions: Blizzard warning in effect

Today, a rapidly intensifying low-pressure system off the coast created classic nor'easter conditions—heavy snow, strong winds, and near-zero visibility. Blizzard warnings are more than just forecasts; they're calls to prepare, to focus, and to rise to the moment. And just like in broadcasting, even if you're scared, you steady your voice, face the storm, and deliver.

—Nick's weather journal

Chapter Fifteen

LIGHTNING IN A BOTTLE

For the sixteenth time today, I'm here to tell you that we've got the perfect week to close out spring. No rain in sight anytime soon and the sun will be shining for everyone. Maybe some time at the beach? I'll be back in ten more minutes to tell you the exact same thing.

–Nick's WMGM-TV broadcast

I always knew I was gay—always. It was a feeling I had even as a kid. I never felt any sort of connection to girls and swear I had a crush on my best friend, Chris, when I was just seven years old. I didn't think much about it until my feelings toward guys intensified significantly in high school, which, I guess, is normal at that age one way or another.

There was a problem, though. I grew up in a very conservative area. I was too young to understand this while living in Brigantine, but when I was forced to move in with my parents in Hammonton, it became apparent that any thought of being in a gay relationship—at least openly—was out of the question.

Hammonton is as deep red as you can get in a predominantly blue state. Ruby red. The majority of people there are old-school Italian

Catholics. Here I was, a gay Jew, and I didn't fit in well. I did everything I could to suppress my feelings for guys and ended up dating girls all through high school, adapting to societal norms and doing what I was "supposed to."

To this day, I could pass as a straight man. I am not flamboyant; I love sports and cars and am more of a "rugged" guy. I've always felt there was some kind of negative stereotype associated with being gay, as if it meant being "girly." It's something I had to work through mentally, but it took a while because I didn't know many gay men to compare myself to. I knew nothing of gay culture beyond the stereotypes.

Over the years, I had a few relationships that felt serious at the time; one even came close to an engagement. I've always had this instinct to try and "fix" people, to take on their pain like it was mine to carry. She came from a fractured home, and there was a lot of turmoil in her life. I wanted to help her find stability, even though I hadn't yet found it in myself.

In truth, we were never truly compatible. Our personalities clashed more than they clicked, but we stayed together for three years, holding on to the hope that love alone would be enough. When it ended, I was crushed—not just by the breakup but by the feeling that I had failed. I couldn't "fix" her life, and for a long time, I took that personally.

It took years to understand that love isn't about rescuing someone; it's about walking alongside them. And healing? That's a journey each person has to choose for themselves.

Afterward, I had one more relationship with a girl. I think I connected more with her family than with her, as was typically the case. She was a very sweet person, but our levels of ambition were completely different. We broke it off after about a year, though we stayed friends.

None of my relationships worked out. Guys often say, "It's not you, it's me" to let girls down easy, but in my case, it truly *was* me. There was no real sexual or emotional connection with any of the girls I dated. I knew it was because I was gay, but I was afraid to admit it. I tried to suppress those feelings as much as I could. I tried to change who I was. And how could I meet a guy in Hammonton, especially after high school?

When I moved out and lived on my own, I thought things might change. I became friends with the owners of the place I was renting, a husband and wife in their sixties. They were born-again Christians who attended church every Sunday. I was never a churchgoer, having grown up as a non-religious Jew.

Robin, the wife, convinced me to go to church with her. It became a weekly affair that I actually looked forward to. We'd grab breakfast beforehand, talk about life, and enjoy each other's company. The church wasn't one of those stuffy, fire-and-brimstone places. They started their services with a rock band—it was cool.

After a while, I started to believe that maybe religion could help me. Maybe, just maybe, it could make me not be gay? I started reading the Bible, praying, and continuing to suppress my feelings for men, hoping they'd disappear. But they never did.

Eventually, I stopped going to church regularly, though I'd attend a Christmas Eve Mass here and there. Around this time, I was working as the closing manager at the Absecon ShopRite. One of my employees, Dan, was the son of my self-scan clerk, Michelle. I adored Michelle. She was friendly, fun, and bighearted.

Dan worked part-time during his college breaks, helping out in the Shop-from-Home department. I always looked forward to seeing him. I thought he was absolutely adorable.

But how could I handle that? I was pretty sure he was gay, but I had no way to confirm it. Plus, I had no game, I was his boss, I wasn't out, and his mom worked for me. It was awkward all around.

One night, a few days before Christmas, the store was a mess. Dan and I were the last ones there, exhausted and ready to go home. As we walked toward the exit, he turned to me and said, "Do you want to grab a drink at Hi Point? My treat."

I didn't drink because of family addiction problems, but I figured I could get a glass of water and use this as an opportunity to connect with him.

"Sure, that would be nice. It's been a long day. I'll meet you over there," I replied.

Hi Point was one of my favorite spots—not for the drinks but for the food. They had the *best* chicken sandwich I'd ever tasted. After a long shift, I was looking forward to grabbing some food.

When I arrived, Dan was waiting in his car. We both got out, sighed collectively, and walked in together. We found seats and were quickly handed menus.

"You hungry?" he asked.

"Sure as hell I am. Haven't eaten since lunch!" I replied.

"Good. Me too. I always get the Chicken BLT—it's soooo good."

"Wait, what? Me too! It's literally the best."

We instantly connected over our favorite sandwich. But was there more to this? Before I could say another word, he startled me by saying, "Sooo . . . I know."

I was confused.

"You know . . . what . . . exactly?" I asked.

"Oh, come on, mister. I know you're gay."

At that moment, I felt a sense of panic *and* relief. Panic because, well, no one knew! And what if he wasn't gay?! That would have been extremely awkward. But I also felt relief because if he *was* gay, I thought I might have a chance with him. Even as hard as it would have been with work, at the very least I'd finally have someone to talk with about this stuff.

"But . . . how?" I asked.

"The way you dress, your eyebrows, your overall vibe. You play the straight guy very well, but I know otherwise. It's OK. I'm gay too."

There it was! I finally had confirmation. I was so excited!

"You are? Would it be inappropriate if I told you I thought you were really cute? I just never—"

"Never knew how to bring it up?"

"Yes. Exactly. It's—"

"Awkward because of my mom?"

"Stop completing my—"

"Sentences?"

I had a perturbed look on my face, but in a playful way. We clearly had some sort of chemistry. I thought maybe I could build on this and it could turn into something? After a few moments of silence, I inched closer over the table.

"Dan, this is all new to me. I'm finally accepting myself, but I've dated girls my entire life. I don't know how to break into the gay world."

"I get it. We don't live in the Gay Mecca of the world, exactly. My boyfriend and I met online."

Ugh! Boyfriend? Damn it! He's taken. I was extremely disappointed, but at least I could still have him as a friend to lean on and ask questions.

"Online? Is there like a Facebook for gay guys?" I joked.

"Well, actually . . . yeah, kinda. It's called Grindr. It's a dating app."

He pulled out his phone, opened up this orange-and-black app, and proceeded to show me all the profiles in our vicinity. I had no idea that was a thing. Online dating was just starting to become more mainstream, and I had heard of success stories before. Maybe that's the way I could meet my special someone?

"That's so cool. I'll download it when I get home. Thanks for showing me."

"Anytime. That's what friends are for."

We kept the conversation going for another hour or so. It was great. It was way past my bedtime, but it was such a refreshing feeling to talk to someone who understood. I found out that he, too, had to pretend to be straight and date girls. Even though there was no prospect of dating him, it was nice to have him as a friend.

We parted ways with a hug, got back in our cars, and away we went. The moment I got home, I downloaded Grindr, set up my profile, and saw who was around. It was 2 AM, so I wasn't going to start a conversation that late. I closed out and went to bed.

The next morning, I woke up to dozens of messages. Some of the pictures guys sent me without even as much as a simple "hello!" would make someone clutch their pearls. Wow. I'd never been exposed to anything like that before. I was interested in having a genuine conversation with someone. I wasn't into the whole hookup culture that was common for kids my age. I wanted something real. I ignored and blocked so many people on the app within just the first few hours.

After a couple of days, the feeling of hope started to fade. Maybe online dating wasn't for me? I wasn't connecting with anyone. Every single guy I talked to for even five minutes wanted the same thing—a quick hookup. No thanks. That wasn't my thing, and I wasn't about to start. I gave it a rest for a bit and focused on work. I was able to occupy my time easily because there was always something going on at the store that needed my attention.

Being a manager at a grocery store is kind of like being a full-time parent. I mean it. There's always something going on—one crisis or disaster after another. It can be overwhelming at times, but you get used to it. Between ShopRite and working in TV, my mind was always moving. I was working for a brighter future and trying to advance in both corporate America *and* in the TV world. I was making significant strides, but it always felt like something was missing.

Professionally, I was in a good place. I had a great-paying job at the store, and I got to live out a dream of mine in TV. But personally, I didn't feel very fulfilled most of the time. Professional accomplishments and accolades are good—don't get me wrong—but I wanted someone to share it all with.

After taking a break from the online dating apps, I decided to try my luck again. It had been a few months, so maybe there were new guys who had signed up and were looking for the same thing I was. One profile caught my attention immediately. His username was "B." He was a cute skater-kid type—thin, glasses, nice hair, and a good smile.

"Hey, I'm Nick! Nice to meet you," I sent over in a direct message.

Crickets. OK. Maybe he didn't check his app often. I continued to go through his profile anyway—5′11, 165, loves traveling and the outdoors. Check, check, and check! A couple of days went by—still nothing. Come on! I thought my profile looked attractive. I'm a pretty normal guy. I guess I'm just not everyone's type?

More unwanted messages came through over the next couple of days. Still no one I connected with. Sigh. I decided I was going to just delete the app and go back to trying to find someone in person. How? Well, I didn't know exactly, but I was batting a thousand, so starting over wouldn't be any worse. Before deleting the app, I messaged "B." again. Why not make one last-ditch effort?

"Hey, hope you're having a great night!"

I sent it along with a couple more photos—one of me on TV and another at work.

I closed out of the app, turned off my phone, and went to bed. The next day was going to be crazy. I had TV at 4 AM and then had to be at the store from two to midnight. Dan Skeldon was on vacation, and it was the week of Easter—so much going on.

I got through my morning shift at the station and made a beeline down Route 9 to get to the store on time. The parking lot was filled to capacity when I got there. I parked out back by the trucks and walked in through the bay doors. My phone vibrated, but I ignored it since I was heading right into the fire. It vibrated again, and again, and then again, but I didn't have the time to check to see who it was.

Dinnertime finally came around. It was always hard to get downtime since the other managers left early, and I was alone for the rest of the shift. I learned to eat *very* quickly. I'd order my food, get it delivered, and retreat to my office with the door closed. I'd instruct the courtesy desk to leave me alone unless the store was burning down, but inevitably, within five minutes, I'd get a call to fix some Karen's coupon issue.

This night was a bit different. I actually had some time to unwind. I bit into my Hi Point Chicken BLT, turned the news on, and sat back. My phone vibrated again. Oh! I totally forgot about it. There were like 9,290,302 notifications.

The first one that caught my eye was from Grindr.

"Hey! I'm so sorry I missed you. Not ignoring you, my father is in the hospital, and it's been rough around here. Heading to a concert. Hope to talk to you later! By the way, my name is Brandon."

He got back to me! I'm *not* hideous! He's interested. Winning! And now I had a name to go off of.

"Hey, Brandon. I'm so sorry to hear about your dad. I hope he has a quick recovery. Don't worry about it—life is crazy for us all. Have fun at your concert. Chat soon!" I replied.

For the first time since downloading the app, the hope that seemed to vanish almost instantly was starting to reappear. My mind was reeling the rest of the night. I started checking my phone every five minutes to see if he responded. I'm sure he wasn't thinking about talking on the app while he was bopping to whatever band he was going to see.

Vibrate.

"Thanks. He's got brain cancer. It's been a journey for us all, but we are getting through it. How's your night?"

"Ugh. I'm so sorry. That must be really hard. It's alright. Wrapping up a long day. How's the concert?"

"It's poppin'. First time seeing Grouplove. One of my favorite bands. Wanna know something? If my sister knew I was talking to you, she'd freak out. She's like obsessed with you. She watches all the time. Obviously, she thinks you're straight LOL."

"Awww, that's fun! I've heard some of their music. Enjoy it. And OMG, really? Small world."

"Yeah, I get to keep a fun secret."

"I don't wanna keep you from the concert, but if you want to text me later, you can." I shared my number.

"I'll text you later."

"OK, cool."

Well, this is amazing! My first genuine connection with someone I thought was attractive and the first conversation that didn't go right to a hookup. I was in a very good mood after that. I felt really bad that he was going through some family health trauma though.

I went through the motions of closing the store, collecting money from the registers, putting back the items people decided last minute they didn't want anymore that piled up at the registers, and making sure everyone was out of the store before shutting off the lights and locking the door. My long day was coming to an end, but I had to be up early the next day to be back on TV, so I'd have to turn in as soon as I got home.

Living only five minutes from the store was a blessing. I didn't have to deal with traffic or driving long distances at night—which, to this day, I absolutely hate because I tend to nod off.

I got home, took a shower, belly flopped into my bed, and turned out the lights. I've always had difficulty sleeping since I was a kid. The tossing and turning is relentless.

As I lay there, looking into the nothingness of my ceiling, all of a sudden it lit up—I forgot to turn off notifications on my phone. Who's texting me at midnight? I reached over to my nightstand and grabbed the phone, looking at it with one eye open.

"Hey, just got home from the concert. I'm sure you're sleeping but wanted to touch base," the text read.

It was Brandon! He didn't forget. While I was exhausted and really needed to get to bed, I also really wanted to talk to him and see how the conversation would go. We ended up texting back and forth nonstop until about three in the morning. When I put the phone down, it was time for me to get up and start my morning routine—oops.

He promised to watch my broadcast at 6 AM—something I didn't expect him to actually do, but it was a sweet gesture. I found my best-pressed white dress shirt, steamed my suit jacket, and stood in the mirror to tie my double Windsor. I was out the door in no time—and on no sleep. I was lucky I was off from the store that day so I could finally catch some time to unwind after leaving the studio.

I lived about twenty minutes from TV40. My morning routine consisted of stopping at the 7-Eleven right next to the studio and grabbing my honey-lemon tea—I've never been a coffee drinker. I'd walk into the building through master control, greet the overnight workers, and walk to my desk, which was all the way in a back corner fairly isolated from everything.

The news started at five, and I was on every ten minutes until eight. That is *a lot* of weather. The hardest days, believe it or not, were when there was nothing going on and we had sun. How many different ways can I tell the people watching that it's going to be nice? It's hard! That day was one of those days. Nothing but high pressure and sunshine.

After my second hit in the six o'clock hour, I looked at my phone.

"Nice tie, dork."

It was a text from Brandon. *OMG, he actually* is *watching.*

After I saw that, I felt like the rest of the morning I was entertaining an audience of one. I even made a reference to Grouplove in one of my forecasts to see if he'd pick up on it—he did.

When the shows were all done, I went back to texting him. This was an adjustment because most of my friends take a half hour to respond to a simple question. Brandon was on top of it. His responses were almost instant. That kept the ball rolling and the conversation lively. I gained the courage to ask him on a date.

"Sooo, what are you doing later? Would you wanna get lunch?" I asked.

"I think that would be cool," he quickly responded. "Where are you thinking?"

"How about Andre's in Brigantine? I grew up there and haven't been in years."

"OK, sounds good to me. Do you want to meet there or carpool?" he asked.

"If you want to meet at Galloway ShopRite, we can just drive together."

"Sweet. I'll see you there around eleven thirty?"

"Works for me. See you then."

Was this really happening? Was I really about to go on a date with a guy? This was a huge first for me. I couldn't exactly tell anyone—I wasn't out of the closet yet. I had no one to share my excitement with, except for Dan. I couldn't wait to tell him all about it when it was over.

I stopped at home, rinsed off, changed out of my suit and into something more casual, hopped in the car, and drove a few minutes down the road to meet Brandon. As luck would have it, he pulled into the spot right next to me. I looked over, waved, and motioned for him to get in.

"Well, it's nice to finally meet you! Good job on the news this morning. I couldn't help but giggle when my sister looked at the TV and said, 'That boy is so hot!'" he said.

"Oh my God, really? That's too funny," I said.

We talked about everything under the sun on our ride over to Brigantine. I learned so much about him in that short period of time. He loved skating, was very handy, enjoyed videography, and was studying to be a mechanical engineer.

It was a beautiful late-spring day. We decided to take advantage of the sun and eat outside. You couldn't have asked for a better day.

The conversation went on for a good two hours. We connected on so many levels. We had genuine chemistry. We talked about him dealing with his father's illness and how that was weighing on him heavily, but he seemed to take it in stride. He learned about my background, my rough childhood, and the fact that I wasn't openly gay. None of those things were a deal-breaker for him.

We wrapped up lunch and then decided to take a walk on the beach to continue talking. It was such a pleasant afternoon. The entire ride home, all I could think was, *I hope he wants to do this again.*

I pulled up in the same spot we'd left from in front of ShopRite. Before I could utter a single word, he said, "I had a lot of fun. Let me know when you're free next and we can hang out. Maybe watch a movie or something?"

"I'd really like that," I replied.

I leaned in for a hug, and we parted ways. I knew at that moment, I'd caught lightning in a bottle.

High temperature: 77°F **Low temperature:** 58°F
Conditions: Mostly sunny with a gentle breeze

Today, the atmosphere was calm—like the kind of day that sneaks up and surprises you with just how beautiful it is. No storms, no pressure, just warmth and light. Sometimes, when you stop trying so hard to control the forecast, the sun shows up anyway.

—Nick's weather journal

Chapter Sixteen

HOLIDAY STORMS & STATION SHOCK

Folks, we've got a big daddy of a storm on the horizon later this week. Could be the biggest snow event in the past five years. If everything comes together JUST the right way, we could be talking over a foot. I'll have more details–up next.

–Nor'Easter Nick, WMGM-TV 40

The holidays are hands down my favorite time of year. Everyone seems so happy. Christmas lights are strung up everywhere, and the overall vibe is optimistic and cheerful. Christmas is the best, and I have a special fondness for this time of year—even though I'm Jewish.

I think it goes back to memories with Bebe. She had a Jewish mother and an Italian Catholic father, so she celebrated both traditions. Our menorah would sit proudly next to the Christmas tree, checking all the boxes.

During the holiday season, ShopRite was especially hectic—long lines, last-minute rushes, and more than a few customer meltdowns. It was chaotic, dramatic, and stressful, but I thrived in it. I had just turned eighteen in September, one of the youngest managers there; I somehow found joy in the madness. Maybe it was the pace, maybe it was the challenge, but it felt like I belonged.

I also loved picking up extra shifts at the TV station. Everyone else wanted time off, but since I didn't have much of a family life, I was eager to cover for my coworkers so they could spend time with their loved ones.

I wanted nothing more than to be on TV as much as possible, so taking on extra work was a no-brainer. Some days, I'd close the store, wake up at 4 AM to do the morning show, return to the store, and then appear on the 6 PM news later that evening.

Eighty-hour workweeks were my norm—I was a workaholic then, and I still am today.

In December 2014, I found out that chief meteorologist Dan Skeldon would be taking a ten-day trip to New England to visit family. It was the holiday season, and I was thrilled; this meant I'd be stepping into the prime-time slot for an extended stretch. For someone still so new to the game, it felt like a huge opportunity—and I was ready to make the most of it. Normally, I worked weekends or the morning show, which meant my exposure was limited. I jumped at the chance to fill in for the highly watched evening broadcasts.

On a cold, gray, and windy morning, I pulled into the parking lot of our WMGM-TV studios. The morning crew had already left, but a few cars were still there. One of them caught my eye—an early-2000s Volkswagen. I recognized it as Dan's.

What's he doing here? I thought. *Shouldn't he be on his way to Rhode Island?*

The icy air bit at my face as I bundled up and walked the fifty feet into the building. Inside, the newsroom was eerily quiet.

Where *is* everyone?

I walked past the control room—no one. Down the sales department hallway—still no one. Even Megan, my news director, had her office door shut. It was odd, especially for this time of day. Usually, I'd get caught in long conversations with coworkers and end up procrastinating. But not today.

After giving up on finding someone to chat with, I headed into the studio. Only one light was on, illuminating the weather desk at the back.

I noticed some movement near the computer and realized I wasn't entirely alone. It was Dan, rummaging through papers, presumably looking for something he'd forgotten before his trip.

"Nor'Easter, what's up? Thanks for filling in for me," he said, glancing up. "I'll be out of your hair in a moment, but I needed to talk to you in person about something important."

He looked uncharacteristically concerned.

"Of course, Dan. Anything I can do for you," I replied. "Is everything OK?"

"Well, not exactly," he said. "We worked really hard to forge a last-minute deal to keep the station open, but it doesn't look like we're going to get the support we need."

"What do you mean 'stay open'? What's going on?"

"Nick, I'm sorry, but our NBC affiliation was pulled. It expired. There was never a concrete contract, and Comcast decided to cut ties. We're closing down on the thirty-first," he said, his voice trembling.

"Oh my God. When did we find this out? What's everyone going to do?"

"We've known this was a possibility for about a year, but we were promised outside groups would step in to help us. We aren't giving up completely, but NBC40 as we know it won't exist by the end of the year," he explained, tears welling in his eyes.

"If you need help finding another TV job, let me know. You're a good kid, and I want to see the best for you."

I stood there, speechless, for several seconds as I tried to process what he had just told me.

"I . . . I . . . I don't know what to say. This is horrible. OK, can we meet after your vacation? I want to discuss some things."

"Yes, of course. I'll be in touch. Have a good week—or at least try to anyway," Dan said as he walked out the door.

I felt a pit in my stomach. A wave of sadness overwhelmed me. Was everything I had worked for my entire life really coming to an end? Was it all crumbling because a greedy corporation didn't want a hyperlocal station competing with their crown jewel in Philadelphia?

I was livid. I didn't even feel like working that night—I was so disgusted and taken aback.

Sure, I had ShopRite. I was in management, earning a good salary at a stable job. But it wasn't my dream. I didn't want to spend my life working at a grocery store. My goal was to work in local TV news, to become a household name, connecting with people every day. Now, that dream felt upended.

I somehow pulled myself together, put my show in sequence, and made it through the night. I wasn't sure how many of my colleagues knew what was happening, and I didn't want to be the one to break the news if they didn't already know. After all, the holiday season was supposed to be joyful. For me now, though, it was anything but.

As I walked to my car, my fake smile faded, and a million thoughts raced through my head.

Do I try to start over in another market?

Who's going to hire someone without a college degree?

Am I going to work at ShopRite for the rest of my life?

What if I pitched ShopRite to let me do a community weather forecast on their social media?

I had a few options in front of me, but no clear direction. With the station set to shut down soon, I chose to make the most of the time left—taking every shift I could and doubling down on a Facebook page I had started a few years earlier as a hobby. I poured energy into it, posting forecast models, casual selfie-style videos, and long-range weather discussions. Social media was on the rise, and I figured it might be an easy way to grow a following. Turns out, it would become a lot more than that.

At first, the page had just a few hundred followers—mostly friends and coworkers from ShopRite. But I plugged it after every forecast, and by the time the station closed, it had grown to over five thousand followers. It was a start. At least I had a way to stay in touch with our viewers.

As the news spread among NBC40 employees, the mood shifted. For many of my colleagues, the station was all they had ever known.

NBC40 was unique—it was a training ground for aspiring journalists. Both Rowan and Stockton universities had journalism programs, and as the local station, we had strong ties to both schools. Many of our staff had started their careers right out of college and stayed for years.

I felt particularly bad for those who didn't want to leave the area and were now forced to find other jobs, some outside the industry entirely. Others managed to transition into related fields, using their communication skills in new ways.

I was still working out my plan.

NBC40 held so many fond memories for me. Dressing up for holidays, acting silly on air, and the friendships we built—it would all be missed. The most devastating part was that the station had been on the air for over five decades, and in the blink of an eye, it would vanish.

Our connection to the community was special. We weren't just a station; we were an extension of the families who watched us.

When the closure became public, one of our lead anchors and producers began working on a documentary to serve as our final broadcast. How they pulled it together so quickly still amazes me.

They asked all on-air talent to record a thirty-second message for the audience. It was an emotional task. I thanked everyone for their loyalty and support and urged them to follow me on social media, promising to continue providing local weather updates online.

New Year's Eve brought it all home. What should have been a night of celebration turned into one of reflection and sadness.

The documentary aired in place of the 11 PM news. It was beautifully produced.

The closing sequence was particularly poignant. It featured all of our farewell recordings, followed by a shot of the empty news desk as Coldplay's "A Sky Full of Stars" played.

One by one, the lights in the studio went out until only the NBC40 logo remained. Then it, too, faded to black.

The end of an era.

The end of my television career—or so I thought.

In the weeks that followed, our team met often. We reminisced about the good times over breakfast or lunch at local restaurants. But the closure hung over us.

I continued to work at ShopRite for another six months. Customers constantly told me how much they missed the station, which only deepened the void.

I worked tirelessly, hoping for a break. In the meantime, I was grateful to have a steady job that allowed me to pursue my passion on the side.

I stayed in close contact with my former news director, Megan Wolf. Together, we brainstormed ways to start another local TV station. Between us, we had connections with influential people who might be able to help.

The station's closure, while devastating, taught me resilience. It pushed me to improve my skills and keep pursuing my dream independently.

Just when I thought my chances of working in television were gone, I got an unexpected call from a man named Frank DiMauro.

High temperature: 42°F **Low temperature:** 28°F
Conditions: Overcast skies, calm winds, dropping pressure

Today, the barometer began to fall steadily—a classic sign that change is on the way. The skies were gray, quiet, uncertain. That's how storms often begin: not with chaos but with stillness. Just because a chapter closes doesn't mean the story ends. Sometimes the hardest pressure drop brings the clearest skies on the other side.

—Nick's weather journal

Chapter Seventeen

BECOMING NOR'EASTER NICK

As we head into New Year's Eve, things will be dark and cold. I wish I had better news for you all. This will be my last broadcast; as you know, we are closing down tomorrow night. It was an honor of a lifetime to bring you the weather every day. Until we meet again, my friends.

—Nick's last WMGM-TV broadcast

To say I was upset and nearly depressed about the closing of NBC40 would be a severe understatement. I had worked so hard for so many years to live out my dream. For five solid years, I got to do just that—but it wasn't enough for me.

I knew what it felt like, what it looked like, and I loved every single moment of it. After experiencing that, it just felt like anything else I did would fall short.

Sure, I had ShopRite, and yes, I was advancing up the corporate ladder, making strides to build my reputation. But that didn't feel special. It felt like I was working a job, not building a career.

I made some amazing friends with coworkers and customers, and the work was rewarding in many ways. Still, there was a feeling of emptiness, like I was letting myself down and not meeting my full potential.

Is this really it? Are my dreams of working in TV really quashed? They can't be. I've come too far, I thought.

To "stay in the game," I decided to transform my living room into a makeshift TV studio. It was just big enough for a large green sheet, a camera, and some lights. It wasn't much, but it was enough to accomplish my vision. Being out on my own gave me tons of flexibility to do as I saw fit without getting in anyone's way.

In my parting message when NBC40 closed, I promised viewers that I would continue providing South Jersey weather through my Facebook page. I was determined to keep that promise.

Back in 2015, the technology wasn't nearly as advanced as it is today, so the quality of my videos wasn't great—but it got the job done. I settled on posting daily morning and evening videos. Using Photoshop and PowerPoint, I went back to my high school roots of creating graphics.

A lot of people tuned in every day, thankful that I was continuing to provide local forecasts. Most NBC40 viewers were fiercely loyal and didn't want to switch to Philadelphia news stations. They felt—rightfully so—that South Jersey didn't receive the coverage it deserved, and our weather was often completely different than that of Philadelphia's. I wanted to fill that void and decided to do everything I could to make it happen.

Over the next six months, my page grew rapidly as more NBC40 viewers began to find and follow me online. I expanded my content to include lunchtime video forecasts and a series of static graphics highlighting weather conditions across different parts of our region. Little by little, what started as a side project was turning into something much bigger.

My local coverage became especially important during the winter as we experienced several major snowstorms. Viewers found comfort in knowing I was there for them, delivering the weather information they trusted.

It was the best of both worlds.

I wasn't working as many hours as I had been when I was essentially full-time at both the station and ShopRite. This gave me time to make a plan for the future and figure out how I would eventually move on from retail.

While I liked what I did, I didn't love it. My grandmother instilled in me the drive to be the best version of myself, and I wanted to honor her.

Working ten hours a day, six days a week, however, wears on you.

After having a taste of my dream job, I wanted more. I had to figure out a way forward, but until that happened, I had to play the hand I was dealt.

Meanwhile, my videos and overall Facebook page became increasingly popular. I started seeing great numbers, and my page grew to ten, fifteen, then twenty thousand followers in just one winter.

I was feeling more confident in my ability to deliver the weather, even without a traditional TV platform—but where did it go from there? The ultimate goal was to get out of retail altogether and focus solely on getting back into broadcast television. How would I make that happen?

The digital space, while it had been around for several years at that juncture, was still new to everyone. Many of us had migrated from MySpace to Facebook, and the way we consumed and disseminated information was starting to change very quickly. But how did that translate to weather broadcasting? That's what I had to figure out—and quick.

After meeting with the owners of Village ShopRite and having them agree to let me do forecasts for the company, I felt a little bit of the push that I desperately needed. It may have been an odd combination —weather and ShopRite—but it made sense at the time, and I had a larger platform for people to see my forecasts. I began creating daily videos that were shared on the stores' Facebook pages. Village ShopRite is the largest franchise in the Wakefern corporation, so we had over twenty-five pages to share to.

When we had big storms on the horizon, I made it a point to email the entire company a very detailed forecast so they could plan shipments from North Jersey and prepare accordingly. I would, in short order, become the go-to guy for all things weather related at ShopRite, and orders were made at my direction when it came to storm impacts, which was incredible. I was grateful for that opportunity.

I started to bolster my video forecasts online with announcements over the intercom in the store. Customers connected the voice with my face and realized I was Nor'Easter Nick from NBC40, and that only helped grow my popularity and support even more.

Within just a few short months after the closure of our TV station, my Nor'Easter Nick Facebook page exploded, and I was looked at as the leader in local weather for our area. People started recognizing me more and more as time went on. I was producing high-quality weather broadcasts from my living room. Given the quality and sophistication, no one would have known where they were being recorded. I felt like I was on my way to living my dream again—but I wanted it to be full-time, not just a side gig.

I never took my eye off the prize. I knew exactly what I wanted and put as many positive vibes as possible into the universe. I knew a thing or two about getting where I wanted to be after essentially having to fend for myself in this world since I was a kid. I continued to grind every day in a job that was acceptable but exhausting, in hopes that someday soon my fortunes would take a turn.

One morning, I received a phone call from an area code I didn't recognize. I don't like talking to people unsolicited, so I let it go to voicemail. I waited a few moments for the voicemail icon to illuminate, put the phone to my ear, and listened to a well-spoken man on the other side.

"Nick, my name is Frank DiMauro. I'm the COO of SNJ Today. We are building a news program, and I've been watching what you do. Would you be available for lunch here in Millville at some point next week? I'd love to connect. Give me a call back when you can."

Were my ears deceiving me? Did that really just happen? A news program? I needed to know more. I was supposed to be in a department manager's meeting in the conference room in five minutes, but this couldn't wait. Something told me this was urgent and could turn into a really, really big deal.

I quietly snuck out of our office, walked down the hall, and looked around as if I were a top-secret spy. I didn't want anyone overhearing my conversation. I dialed the number the man left, and it rang and rang and rang some more. I almost lost hope, but at the very last second, he answered.

"Hi, Nick! Thanks so much for calling me back," he said.

"Frank, I really appreciate you reaching out. How did you find out about me?" I asked.

"I've been in the media business for a long time, and I know talent when I see it. I used to watch you on TV40 and then saw you pop up as a suggestion on Facebook. What you're doing is incredible. We should meet," he replied.

I was flabbergasted. This came out of the blue, totally unprompted. Had all the years of believing in the universe and positive energy paid off? It made me really believe in the teachings of *The Alchemist.*

"Well, I can't thank you enough! My goal is to get back into television, and I would absolutely love the chance to meet with you. I'm off on Wednesdays. Does that work for you?" I said, clearly excited.

"Twelve PM, lunch at Antoinette's in Millville. Next Wednesday. See you there."

"Great! See you there. Thanks again."

Positive thoughts raced through my mind for the next several days.

I couldn't help but feel as though my calling was finally here. It all felt incredibly motivating, and I started to see a light at the end of the tunnel.

Truth be told, I hadn't done many interviews. I had the initial interview when I got the job pushing carts at fifteen, then at NBC40 a couple of years after that, and finally when I had promotions at ShopRite—but those were friendly and with people I had already known. This meeting with Frank was a big deal for me, as it was the first time I was going to meet with someone in a professional setting, tell them about my life, and explain how my skills could help their endeavors.

For the next few days, I went over things in my head. I was preparing as best I could to meet Frank. There was a lot riding on this interview, so I wanted to make sure it was as perfect as possible.

I couldn't stop thinking about what the future could bring. I kept imagining how much my life would change if I were to get this job. If the offer was right, I'd even have the chance to leave ShopRite, which, in and of itself, was a scary thought because it was all I had ever known. It was my safety net.

I didn't tell anyone aside from Brandon about this meeting because I didn't want word getting out to any of my bosses at corporate. I also didn't want to jinx anything because I'm a bit superstitious that way. It was extremely difficult for me to keep it under wraps because I cannot keep a secret. If the Russians kidnapped me and told me they'd torture my entire family if I said anything—I'd still probably cave. So, this was a big deal for me to stay quiet.

The day arrived. I got up early as usual, took my shower, pressed my shirt, practiced my interview a little more, and was on my way out the door. Millville was about an hour from my house, and I wanted to make sure I was there early. My grandmother always told me, "If you're not five minutes early, you're late." That mentality sticks with me to this day.

I had never been to Millville before that day. I never really had a reason to take the trek deep into the heart of Cumberland County, but little did I know it would end up becoming one of the most important trips of my career.

After five minutes of driving around in circles, I finally found the restaurant and a parking spot about a half block down the street. Parallel parking is not my favorite maneuver, but I managed to do the deed. I'll never forget the beads of sweat forming on my forehead as I thought about the implications this meeting could have. I tried my best to slow my breathing as I approached the restaurant.

I was looking down at my phone to confirm the date, time, and location, as though it were going to magically change, when I heard a voice call to me: "Nick! Over here!"

I looked up and saw a distinguished man with curly hair; a long, beige peacoat; and a welcoming smile. He extended his hand.

"Nice to meet you. I'm Frank. Let me get the door for you. I'm starved, and this place has some of the best food in the area," he said.

"Thank you for your time, Frank. I've been looking forward to meeting you since you called me last week," I replied.

We sat at a table for four by the large picture window overlooking High Street.

"Ken is running a few minutes late, but we can order an app in the meantime. So tell me about yourself. How did you get into media, and how are you so young?" Frank asked inquisitively.

Ken, the owner of the TV station, would be joining us for lunch that day.

"Well, Frank, honestly, I knew when I was just six years old that I wanted to do this. I had a bit of a rough childhood but always kept my eye on the prize. I've always known I was put here to do something big, but I'm not quite sure what yet. I do know I want to be in TV, and I think my experience and ability to connect with viewers would make me a great asset to what you're doing," I said, going straight for the gold.

Frank had a look of almost disbelief as I went deeper into my background. He asked many questions, and we exchanged stories about our time in the media. It turned out he had been an executive at one point with HBO and had worked in all types of high-level positions throughout his career. I thought it was absolutely amazing that he was bringing that talent to South Jersey to create something new.

Within a few minutes of us talking, we heard the bell perched above the entrance door ring. In walked a short, gray-haired man, about fifty. He stopped by the hostess booth to ask where we were and then noticed us sitting by the window. I leapt up out of my seat, extended my hand, and introduced myself.

Ken sat down and immediately dove into his mission.

"Nick, Frank called this meeting today because we are looking to build something revolutionary in this area. Something new. Something never before done in this region. There is too much negativity in the news these days, and we think if we introduce positive news, we can change the game," he said, clearly very excited about the prospects.

Now, I have to be honest. My immediate thought was, *This is never going to work. I love the idea, but people want hard news. People want death, destruction, and the weather.* But as he kept talking, I became more intrigued.

"We want you to be a part of this. We've been watching you for some time, and we think you'd be the right person to lead the weather department."

Those words meant so much to me. I felt like I was given a new lease on my career. Positive vibes were flowing all over the place.

"Nick, I'm not a media guy, but I believe in surrounding myself with people who are experts in what they do. My background is in equipment rental. We've been very successful, but it hasn't been fulfilling. I want to make a difference in people's lives, and that's why I'm starting this TV station. It is sorely needed."

The man had heart. He was doing this for the right reasons, and I absolutely wanted in. How could I express that but also get paid what I knew I was worth? I got paid peanuts at NBC40, and ShopRite took care of me. I couldn't possibly accept anything less than what I was making as a manager there.

The meeting went on for a good hour and a half as we laughed and learned more about one another. I was invited back to their headquarters to tour the studio that was in the process of being built. The building was extremely historic and had been the home of many businesses over the years. It started out as a glass factory, then became one of Coca-Cola's main office spaces, and now it would become a TV station. Cool!

We spoke for another hour at their office and agreed to keep communication open and ongoing. As I was getting ready to walk back to my car, Ken shook my hand, pulled me close, and whispered in my ear: "Whatever it takes to get you on board, we will do."

I thanked Ken and Frank for their time and scurried back to my car for my long journey home. I was absolutely elated. The meeting could not have gone any better. I was told they would submit an offer via email in the coming days. All I could think about was starting over and doing what I loved. This felt good. This felt real.

By the end of the week, I received an email from Frank asking me to give him a call to discuss a plan to move forward. I wasted absolutely no time and called him right away.

"Nick! Thanks for getting back to me so soon. We talked it over and really want to get you on board. We are going to be building a whole team and want your help in putting everyone together. What will it take to get us to a place we can agree on that will be good for both of us?" he asked.

I knew this was a make-or-break situation for me. I couldn't undervalue myself, and I knew this could be my way out of ShopRite.

"Frank, I am absolutely honored you want me to be a part of it. I believe in what you're doing and think we could build something really incredible together. And yes, I'd love to help you build the team! I'm currently making about seventy grand a year, and I've got full health care to go along with that. I would need you to match or come close to that in order for me to leave ShopRite," I said confidently.

"Consider it a deal. I'll have Donna, my assistant, send over the paperwork in the morning. Welcome to the team! I have to go, but I'll be in touch soon!"

The other end of the line went silent.

What just happened? I kept asking myself. I think I even pinched my arms multiple times to make sure I was actually awake. My jaw was stuck open. I was so shocked. This *was* real. It *was* happening, and my life was about to change forever as a result. Nor'Easter Nick was back.

When I got to work later that afternoon, I made it a point to get my store manager, Charlie, alone in his office to discuss my future plans. I was hesitant at first because we were thick as thieves, and I had become his right-hand man in the two years I worked at the Galloway store. I didn't want to disappoint him by telling him I was leaving, but it was a conversation that needed to be had.

I walked up the steps, down the hall, and into our office. He was sitting there looking at his computer with a scowl on his face—which meant Charlie was not having a good day. I closed the door behind me, he looked up, and we chatted for a good twenty minutes about my decision to move on.

When it was over, he told me: "I knew we weren't going to keep you forever, kiddo. Thank you for all you've done for me and the store. You're going to be great out there on TV, and I can't wait to watch you every night."

Most people give two weeks' notice. I gave Charlie over a month's notice so we could plan to replace me, and I would train whomever our district manager decided to promote to take my position. My departure was bittersweet, but it was nice to have the support of everyone

I had worked with for so many years. Some of my colleagues banded together and threw me a "retirement" party at a local restaurant on my final night. It was really touching. To this day, I stay in close contact with many of the people I worked with.

It was time to start the next chapter of my life and really build the Nor'Easter Nick brand.

High temperature: 66°F **Low temperature:** 49°F
Conditions: Mostly cloudy with clearing skies and rising pressure

Today, a departing low gave way to high pressure, clearing the skies and bringing a sense of calm after days of turbulence. Sometimes you have to weather the storm to find the next front pushing in—one that brings clarity, purpose, and momentum. Change doesn't always feel comfortable at first, but it almost always brings new light.

—Nick's weather journal

Chapter Eighteen

CORPORATE STORM

We've got a whirlwind week ahead. Ups and downs with perhaps some unexpected twists by the weekend. Temps will be all over the place, and we've got several chances of precip. Definitely a week you need to pay close attention to!

—Nick's SNJ Today broadcast

The SNJ Today model was different. First and foremost, the content was starkly different from what you'd see on other TV news stations that only cared about death and destruction—we focused on *positive* news. Like I said, different. It was a refreshing break from network news for sure, but personally I wasn't confident about the long-term viability. I would ultimately be right about those feelings a few years down the road.

At NBC40 we had our own channel. We could run whatever content whenever we wanted, and everyone knew when to tune in. We had programming and shows all day. That station was a staple in our community. SNJ Today did not own any broadcast signal so we had to be creative on how to get our content out there to the public.

While there were significant strides being made in the digital space at the time, the world was not ready to go fully in that direction just yet. We still needed the traditional broadcast component. Ken and Frank met with Comcast several times to the point of exhaustion trying to get them to OK the use of the WMGM-TV 40 signal for our broadcasts. They tried and tried and then tried some more, but Comcast would not budge. Why? Because we were a threat. It was the very same reason they stripped the affiliation from NBC40 in the first place.

At the time, Comcast had acquired NBC—and with that came a shift in priorities. They wanted full control over revenue and viewership, funneling everything toward their owned and operated station in Philadelphia. O&O stations are directly owned by the network itself, unlike affiliates that may carry the same programming but operate independently. Comcast had no interest in allowing an independent station like ours to compete with their flagship property. So they blocked us at every turn—limiting access, resources, and support. It was clear: Protecting profits mattered more than serving the communities that relied on us.

Ken and Frank were finally able to get onto a broadcast channel, circumventing the process by partnering with WACP-TV, which was based out of Winslow, New Jersey. They aired 24/7 on channel 4, but their content was horrible. Infomercials all day long. Nothing that actually gave people a reason to watch.

It was a win-win situation for all parties. We would produce quality content to bring people to the channel, and we'd have a home where our news could be watched each night. There were a couple issues with the model though. First, it was expensive. They agreed to pay a quarter of a million dollars each year for us to air our news. Second, with WACP being an infomercial network, it would be hard to direct people to the channel because if they went early they'd just see the ShamWow guy. Why would they think there was anything more to it?

I ran into problem number two all the time. In my adventures around the area, I'd talk to hundreds of people a week. I'd say two-thirds said the same thing: "I wish there was more content on the channel. We try to watch the news but we honestly forget it's on there."

That message coming from a couple people really wouldn't have been a big deal, but when hundreds say the same thing, there's an issue. And I agreed with them. If we were given access to the WMGM signal, we would not have had this problem whatsoever. But we carried on. We made it work with what we had.

I noticed things getting tight by year two. Advertising revenue was greatly outweighed by expenses, and a huge expense was paying for being on air on a channel frankly most people just were not watching.

Cognizant of that fact, I wanted to do what I could to preserve not only the future of our station, but, selfishly, my own future. I left a very stable—albeit not the best—job to take the leap into TV full-time. I needed this to work.

I wrote up an entire business plan by 2018 to shift our focus away from WACP that detailed line by line how to be more successful by switching to fully digital. We could do *more* news, produce *more* content, and get *more* eyes on our stuff for way cheaper. Saving $250K a year would cover almost half of the salaries.

My strategy was well thought out and comprehensive. It was about ten pages long and I was extremely proud of it. I think my experience as a retail manager helped in the creation of the business plan because I was very well versed in dealing with budgets.

I made a plan to meet with Frank over lunch and discuss my proposal. We ended up at a local BBQ joint in Millville one afternoon.

"Alright, Nick, what do you have for me?"

"Frank, I know we've got some financial issues. I'm aware that our sales team isn't exactly very strong and leads are falling flat. The station cannot sustain itself on what I'm bringing in alone. WACP is killing us with what we give them each year . . ." I said very confidently.

"You're very observant. And you're right. We do have some issues that we need to figure out. I would have thought by year two we'd be profitable, but we are in the red. We need to right the ship."

"I've got a plan to go fully digital. Look here." I reached into my backpack and pulled out my report. "We can turn a profit by cutting costs and increasing the number of sponsors we bring on. All it takes is creating affordable, appealing packages. People just don't want to pay three hundred dollars a spot to be on a channel nobody's watching. At least with digital we know we can get the eyes."

"How long did this take you? This is so well done. I've seen a lot of business plans, and this is right up there with the best."

"A couple days. I just want this to work. Do you think Ken can be convinced?"

"That's the issue. I don't think so. He is so stuck on this idea that the news needs to be on TV. It's going to be a hard sell no matter how much we say he will be able to make," he responded in an almost melancholy way.

"Just promise me you'll try? I know we could be very successful if we went digital. The world is changing. We could get literally every aspect of our newscast sponsored. It's very expensive for these small businesses to pay for the TV product, especially if it's not working for them. The digital platforms *would* work for them. I know it. Weather alone! Let's push."

"OK, OK! I get it. I agree with you. I'll see what I can do. I'm meeting with him one-on-one later in the week and I'll propose the idea. I'll keep you in the loop."

If there was anyone I could talk to about this stuff, it was Frank. He understood my perspective, and I knew *he* was movable.

That following Monday, I stopped in his office like I did pretty much every day.

"Soooooooo, how'd the convo with Ken go?" I asked.

He looked at me, glanced toward the door, and said, "Close the door."

From that alone I knew I wasn't going to get the news I wanted.

"I did my best, Nick. I really did. He won't budge. He really thinks this is going to end up working. We are going to adjust the model though. We are going to start doing hard news by the first of the year. Maybe that will be the jolt we need."

"I get it. Maybe the format change will help us, but I really do still believe that going digital would save us," I said.

"Let's be optimistic. I know we need big changes or this isn't going to work out."

High temperature: 54°F **Low temperature:** 39°F
Conditions: Breezy with increasing clouds

Today started off crystal clear—but by late afternoon, clouds quietly crept in and covered the sky, unnoticed by most until the light began to dim. That's the thing about change: You don't always see it coming until it's already settled. The world of news is no different. The storm wasn't the death of television—it was the rise of digital, building in the background. I saw the front approaching, but not everyone was ready to read the radar. Sometimes you prepare, sometimes you push through, and sometimes you just have to wait for the next weather pattern to bring clarity.

—Nick's weather journal

Chapter Nineteen

NORTH STAR

A winter weather advisory goes into effect this evening for a storm that could bring some dangerous travel conditions around the evening rush. If you don't need to be outside later on, stay home. I'll have more on this coming up in just a bit.

–Nick's SNJ Today broadcast

It was a really exciting time in my life. Frank and Ken asked my advice on additional hires. The first two people I recommended right off the bat were Megan Wolf and Cara Velardi—two amazingly talented women who were masters of their craft and would be a tremendous asset to what we were about to do. They were brought in for interviews and hired. I was ecstatic.

We moved on to sports and news. In the sports department, they decided on Mike Frankel—whom I worked weekends with at NBC40. Mike was charismatic, fun, and most important—a solid worker who strove for perfection.

The final piece of the puzzle was our lead anchor. Several candidates were interviewed, but one woman stood out: Cara McCollum. Cara was a former Miss New Jersey, and her talent was bursting at the seams. Before too long, we had our news team put together, and we were getting ready to launch our weekly newscast.

The first few episodes were rough. We were all trying to find our way through it, as it was a different format than any of us were used to. There were adjustments that needed to be made, but once we worked out the kinks, we were ready to expand and increase the frequency at which the show was produced.

Within just two months, we launched our nightly newscast, which came with tons of support from the community. South Jersey residents were fiercely loyal to TV40 and were devastated when we closed at the end of 2014. We were a station that had existed for over four decades and provided real, unfiltered, and unbiased local news coverage. I don't think the area ever recovered from that void, nor do I think it ever will.

In addition to my weather duties, I was tasked with helping the station with sales. Now, let me tell you—I absolutely *hate* sales. I only agreed because I wanted to see our station succeed. The area needed it, and personally, I needed it.

To this day, I find selling incredibly uncomfortable, even though I'm good at it. I've never been a fan of the feeling of begging someone for money. It just doesn't feel natural to me. Cold-calling people? Showing up at a business unannounced? Awkward!

There was one thing going for me that most salespeople didn't have—people knew who I was. It was an instant icebreaker.

The number of relationships I built over the course of working at SNJ Today is invaluable. Many of those relationships blossomed into friendships that I maintain to this day. To say it was a difficult start is putting it mildly. We were confronted with money problems almost immediately.

The station's ownership had budgeted for commercial prices that were far beyond what we were charging at NBC40. We had customers who were paying as low as twenty-five dollars a spot. At NBC40, we owned the station and could put their commercials anywhere. That was a luxury we didn't have at SNJ Today because we didn't own the actual station we were running our newscast on. We were renting the airwaves, which made things quite complicated.

I can't fault the ownership. They just didn't fully understand the news business. They came from a totally different background.

The whole SNJ Today model was built on the idea that we were going to secure contracts from customers who would pay $300 for a single commercial spot. I don't even think customers paid that to be on a Philadelphia newscast.

Now, take my discomfort of selling to people and combine it with me asking them for thousands and thousands of dollars to advertise on a television station no one had ever heard of. You see the problem, right?

Within a few months, it became apparent we just were not going to meet those expectations, so the model changed. While we remained on the air and delivered television newscasts, we changed our focus to be more digital oriented. Honing in on producing content for social media, our website and app was a little less expensive and helped save money to fund things short term. I sold as much TV as possible, but certainly not at the prices we had originally advertised.

At that point, we all figured that *any* money was good money. Looking back on it, I wish I had been more involved and vocal. We may still be running that station today—who knows?

We provided a resource for people to believe in and trust. We were at every press conference and every major story while keeping positivity as our guiding principle.

Megan Wolf, a total and complete professional, was leading the news division and did an absolutely incredible job. I have never, in the over a decade I've known her, seen her mix her personal views into the news. She always made sure the newscasts were as balanced as humanly possible and was always sure to get both sides of a story before running it—the way news should be done. It's important that people are given the facts and only the facts when it comes to local news. Let the viewers decide how they feel. It is not the job of the media to tell people how to think or feel. Megan understood that, and we were a much better organization as a result.

The company continued to grow and expand in all directions—perhaps a little too fast—but we all felt we were in a good situation.

Something that is rare in the news industry is having management that actually cares about their employees. From the top down, we had great relationships. Everyone did their job to the best of their ability, showed respect, and contributed to our overall success.

Boundaries were respected and everyone was generally happy—again, this is a rarity in local news.

Within a year of the station being open, I felt we were really hitting our stride. We opened up marketing and production companies under the SNJ Today umbrella. It was really nice to be a part of something larger than myself.

We had a tremendously talented crew, and we were all living our best lives—until tragedy struck.

It was mid-February, just before Valentine's Day. I was forecasting a freak ice storm that was set to make travel extremely difficult.

We did the newscast for the day and went our separate ways. It took forever for me to get home. I lived about an hour away from the station at the time; this trip took me every bit of two hours.

Everything was normal that night. My partner, Brandon, and I ate dinner, did a little work, went to the gym, watched a show, and went to bed—the stuff I did every single night. Nothing out of the ordinary.

I think it was around three in the morning when my phone rang. I ignored it once, thinking it was just an accidental dial.

It rang a second time. I still ignored it.

On the third ring, I grabbed my phone and opened my eyes just enough to see that it was Megan calling.

What could she possibly want at that hour?

My immediate reaction was that I forgot to do something and my weathercast didn't post overnight.

This was a little more common for me since my memory is horrible—everyone knew it.

I answered.

"Hello! What did I forget now?" I asked groggily.

There were a few seconds of silence.

"Hello?" I asked again.

Megan finally answered. She sounded very shaken. I knew instantly that this was much bigger than me forgetting to do something.

"Nick, Cara McCollum was in an accident after work, spun off the road, and she's in critical condition at the ICU. That's all we know at the moment, but I will be in touch when we have more information."

My heart sank into my stomach. The feeling of darkness overcame my whole body, and I couldn't move for several minutes as I tried to process what I'd just been told.

At that point, it was impossible to go back to sleep. I paced around the house, hoping and praying for some positive news.

Brandon had been up late finishing work the night before so I felt bad bothering him, but I needed someone to talk to so I woke him up. We sat on the edge of the bed and I told him the news. We were both at a loss for words. He gave me a hug and I told him to go back to bed. I went downstairs to make a cup of tea.

The next phone call I received certainly wasn't the news I wanted to hear. Cara passed away at just twenty-two years old.

She had the world at her fingertips. She was beautiful, intelligent, and a difference maker. She would have gone on to work for national news—I am certain of that.

We decided not to have a newscast that day—but we all met at the station regardless. Mike Frankel worked on a very touching tribute to Cara's life that we ran in her honor in place of the news.

I'll never forget watching that piece. It was so well done.

We all had only known Cara for about a year, but we felt as though it were a lifetime.

I had never experienced a tragedy like that in my life before.

Year after year, the anniversary of her passing comes around, and year after year we smile a little brighter for having known her and had her in our lives.

Cara's legacy lives on in the form of her nonprofit work, providing books to kids in need so they can explore the world through literature. She will never be forgotten for all she contributed to our area.

The difficult decision to replace her was on the table.

It was something we had to come to terms with, but it was incredibly uncomfortable.

We had several team meetings in the weeks after her passing to discuss it. Several people filled in until the decision was made.

The station's ownership decided on longtime NBC40 lead anchor Michelle Dawn Mooney to take the reins.

Michelle is one of the most professional anchors I have ever had the pleasure of working with. Her ability to deliver the news passionately without bias in any situation is unparalleled.

It was nice to be reunited with her.

Our team was complete once again, but there would forever be a void left by Cara's absence.

High temperature: 40°F **Low temperature:** 28°F

Conditions: Icy with freezing rain

Today, a thin sheet of ice coated everything—slick, dangerous, and unexpected. Ice storms can bring life to a sudden halt, just like tragedy. They remind us how fragile and unpredictable life can be. One moment we're cruising forward, and the next, we're spinning off course. But even in the darkest of winters, memories—like sunshine—help thaw the pain.

—Nick's weather journal

Chapter Twenty

CHOSEN TIES

It's not gonna be the BEST day out there—you can choose to stay inside or throw on a pair of jeans and a coat and head out shopping. Look for some PM showers so have those umbrellas handy. You can choose to stay indoors and watch a movie though—that may be my choice!

—Nick's Facebook Broadcast

When Brandon and I started dating, I was determined to make a good impression on his family. The problem was, I had no idea what kind of people they were. Like any self-respecting investigator in the age of social media, I did the only logical thing: I stalked his mom, Mary Jo, on Facebook. What I discovered left me both awestruck and terrified.

Mary Jo was a bodybuilder. Not just someone who dabbled in fitness, but a full-on, flexed-biceps, gym-dedicated powerhouse. Her profile was filled with photos of her lifting weights that looked heavier than my car and smiling with an intensity that could scare off a bear. As someone who had never touched a dumbbell unless it was to move it out of the way, I was intimidated, to say the least. How was I supposed to make a good impression on a woman who could probably bench-press me?

The first time Brandon told her about us, she was . . . skeptical. Not about me as a person but about my age. Apparently, she took one look at me in the photos Brandon showed her and said, "He's way older than you, isn't he?" When Brandon assured her I wasn't, she asked him to verify it. That's right—she asked for my ID. To her credit, it wasn't meant to be mean-spirited. She was just being protective of her son, and honestly, I respected it. Still, I couldn't help but feel a little embarrassed.

She had watched me on television each morning, and I guess she didn't think someone so young would be doing that job.

At the time, I was still working at ShopRite, and the only scanner we had was at work, in the department managers' office. So, there I was, scanning my driver's license and sending it over to Brandon to pass along to his mom. Looking back, it was probably one of the most ridiculous things I've ever done for a relationship. But hey, it worked. Mary Jo confirmed that I was, in fact, the age I claimed to be, and I passed her first test.

Meeting her in person was nerve-wracking, but once I got past the initial intimidation factor, Mary Jo turned out to be one of the kindest, most welcoming people I've ever met. She didn't just accept me into their family; she made me feel like I had always been a part of it. She has this way of making everyone feel important and loved, like you matter just by being in her presence.

Brandon has two sisters, Britney and Brielle, who were just as warm and welcoming. We clicked instantly, bonding over our shared sense of humor and love for late-night snacks. They treated me like one of their own from day one, and it felt like I'd gained two new best friends overnight.

But the family dynamic wasn't without its scars. Brandon's father had passed away the year before from brain cancer, and his absence was a palpable void in their lives. Mary Jo had stepped up in ways that most people couldn't even imagine, becoming both the emotional anchor and the pillar of strength for her children. It was clear that their bond as a family had deepened through their shared grief, and they had a resilience that was both inspiring and humbling.

Despite the heartache, the love in that household was undeniable. They laughed, cried, and argued like any family, but there was an undercurrent of unconditional support that I had never experienced before. For someone like me, who had always felt like an outsider in family settings, being a part of theirs was nothing short of transformative.

Mary Jo, Britney, Brielle, and even Brandon himself showed me what it meant to be truly accepted and loved. They didn't just let me in; they embraced me with open arms. And for the first time in my life, I felt like I belonged, which was an incredible feeling.

There was a brief period of time when I moved in with Brandon at his childhood home. Mary Jo had moved out and the house just sat there dormant, so we figured it would be a great opportunity for us to have tons of space to ourselves and practice for when we'd have a home that was actually ours.

While it was a nice place with beautiful vaulted ceilings and large areas to host people, it was very inconvenient for work. That year I had committed to leaving ShopRite and working for SNJ Today full-time. The station was based in Millville, and we lived in Galloway, which, on a good day with no traffic, was just north of an hour and ten minutes away. There was no direct route; we had to go all along the back roads.

Even though Brandon was attending Rutgers for engineering, his passion was always media. He loved everything about TV production. I ended up getting him a job at the station. So we both worked there, but at different times of the day. He was one of our camera guys so he was all over the state collecting footage. Carpooling wasn't an option with us, but I did end up striking a deal with our anchor, Michelle. We would take turns driving since she only lived a few miles from us. It turned into a tenable situation for us over the course of a few months once we had all the details hammered out.

It was still exhausting—especially during times of bad weather. I'll never forget the one (and only) snowstorm we drove through to get home. It took nearly three hours traveling at twenty-five miles per hour. That was a trip I would not do again.

We talked about moving closer to Millville to be able to get to work quicker and have less stress. It came at just the right time, too, as Mary Jo decided to sell the family home and take advantage of the equity that was built up in the house over the past twenty years. She made sure she didn't sell until we were completely ready.

Brandon and I found our first apartment a couple towns over. It wasn't glorious, but it was a place we could finally call ours. We quickly learned the responsibility of paying rent and utility bills. For the first time we both felt like real adults.

High temperature: 69°F **Low temperature:** 51°F
Conditions: Breezy with early morning sunshine fading to overcast

Today's sky started bright but gradually clouded over—yet even through the shifting light, the warmth stayed. It reminded me that not all change is bad. Sometimes the winds shift and bring you into a new season of life—one where you find belonging in unexpected places.

Like moving into a home that isn't yours, only to realize it feels more like home than any you've known. Love, like weather, doesn't always arrive how or when you expect it—but when it does, you'll know.

—Nick's weather journal

Chapter Twenty-One

A NEW FRONT

And this will be my final forecast as SNJ Today will be closing down operations tonight. Thank you all for your kind words and support. You can catch me online for your latest local forecast around the clock!

—Nick's final SNJ Today broadcast

While things seemed to be going in a positive direction, when we were roughly three years into the existence of SNJ Today, I started seeing the writing on the wall that perhaps it wasn't the most stable model. Sales slowed down, fewer people were interested in advertising with us because of the type of news we covered—mostly positive, feel-good stuff—and we were airing at probably the worst time of the day: 7 PM.

Competing with other TV stations wasn't an issue because people had a strong sense of loyalty to a South Jersey–only newscast. Every other station was Philadelphia-based and focused their coverage on the city and the suburbs immediately outside of the city, rarely stepping foot into our region. So our coverage was not an issue—it was the time slot.

Jeopardy! just so happened to air at the same time. We saw it in the ratings; many more folks opted to watch a game show they were familiar with and forego watching our nightly broadcast. This became a huge pain point for us and something that we couldn't recover from as hard as we tried. Without sales, the owner was stuck footing the bill for the entire operation. No smart businessperson is going to do that for an extended period.

I was heartbroken when I came to the realization that the project that so many of us worked so hard on would likely fade away into the abyss. We continued for about another year before it started becoming apparent to more people that the station likely wouldn't be around for much longer.

The final days of SNJ Today were a whirlwind of emotions, challenges, and the relentless pursuit of a vision. SNJ Today had been more than just a local TV station. In the four short years it was in existence, it became a community pillar that told the positive stories of Southern New Jersey, connecting neighborhoods, amplifying local voices, and providing essential information. But as the curtain began to close on this chapter, I found myself at a crossroads, determined to keep the spirit of local storytelling alive—a very common theme over the course of my career, it seems.

When SNJ Today announced its impending closure, I couldn't sit idly by. The region needed a platform—something modern, digital, and agile—to fill the void that SNJ Today's absence would create. Partnering with our lead anchor, Michelle, whose passion for local news mirrored mine, seemed like the natural next step. Together, we began to craft a vision for a digital-only TV station that would be more than a replacement; it would be a reinvention.

I had planned all along to go out on my own and focus on the weather only. That was a no-brainer. I already had businesses committed to advertising on my Facebook page. At the time I had about fifty thousand followers, and it was an appealing platform for companies to use to get their message out to tons of local viewers.

Michelle and I would constantly brainstorm how we could improve SNJ Today on our hour-long journey to work. Michelle had been in local news for two decades and had seen a lot.

"If only we were in charge. This whole thing would be turned around, you know?" she said out of the blue one day.

When it came time for the station to close, we had some deep conversations and mapped out a plan to create our own thing.

"What would we call it? It would have to be a name that was representative of where we are and what we are doing, something with TV in the name, right?" she said.

"How about SJN-TV? After all, I've always thought that's what SNJ Today should have been called all along," I responded. SNJ stood for "Southern New Jersey Today," but "South Jersey News"—SJN—just had a better ring to it. It flowed off the tongue much easier.

"SJN-TV. I like that."

"I'll talk to Brandon tonight and start coming up with some logo designs for us to look at."

Brandon was always a visionary and could take an idea we told him verbally and turn it into a digital masterpiece. I was able to accomplish my mission by the end of the night with several logos to choose from. He even started working on some renderings for a potential set.

The wheels were set in motion nearly a month before SNJ Today closed. As soon as Frank told me we were closing, I went into fight-or-flight mode. I decided fighting was the much better option. We were on our way to Key West on vacation, and I spent every moment of downtime connecting with advertisers that supported us at SNJ Today and NBC40. I had several commitments, so I knew at least our bills and mortgage would be covered. I knew after the station closed we'd have a good springboard for the future. I was personally satisfied, but I wanted more. I wanted to continue to serve the community through avenues above and beyond the weather.

The first step was developing a comprehensive business plan. I didn't have to start from the very beginning because I had the business plan I wrote a little over a year prior to try and save SNJ Today. It outlined from soup to nuts how to run a digital-only station. The fiscal plan and budget were solid, and the best part was that it was all very achievable with local sponsorships priced at exactly the right level. I felt confident that investors and potential sponsors would easily buy into our plan.

The next step was reaching out to local businesses again. Some I had already convinced to advertise on my new weather platform; others were conversations started from scratch. I drafted emails, made calls, and knocked on doors, pitching our vision to anyone who would listen. I met with restaurant owners, local chambers of commerce, car dealerships, and even small boutique shops. Each conversation was a blend of storytelling and strategy, painting a picture of a digital platform that could offer affordable advertising and real community engagement. While some were skeptical, others saw the potential and agreed to exploratory meetings. Those initial conversations laid the groundwork for a network of potential advertisers and supporters.

Beyond businesses, I also reached out to local organizations and educational institutions. Colleges were particularly receptive to the idea, seeing value in a partnership that could provide internships and exposure for media students. Building these relationships was vital; our new station couldn't succeed in isolation—it had to be deeply embedded in the community.

We were extremely close to forging an agreement with Stockton University, which not only had a television program but also studio space and a local channel that covered most of Atlantic County and a portion of Cape May County. It was even a smaller footprint than we had at NBC40, but it was something we could work with. We dug our heels in and pursued that option relentlessly.

As our plans began to take shape, finding the right office space for the station became a priority. We wanted a location that was accessible, modern, and flexible enough to house a state-of-the-art digital studio. After weeks of searching, we zeroed in on a space in the heart of Atlantic City. It was a bright, open-concept office with enough room to set up a newsroom, a green-screen studio, and even a small podcast area. Walking through the empty space, Michelle, Megan, Brandon, and I could already envision the bustling energy it would hold: anchors preparing for live streams, editors piecing together stories, and the hum of cameras capturing it all.

The best part of it all? It was in a building owned by friends of ours. They were willing to work with us on construction needs and cut us a deal on rent. To me and Megan it was *the* perfect place. We thought for years that NBC40 and then later SNJ Today should have been headquartered in Atlantic City, since it was the "major city" of the area. We had the perfect opportunity to build our dream station there.

I met with the president of the Casino Reinvestment Development Authority (CRDA), which was basically in charge of city improvement projects. I maintained a close relationship with the marketing director for the agency and he was all in on helping us, since he was a big fan of local news and the idea of having us in Atlantic City.

It would have been the perfect scenario for us and the cheapest solution, as the CRDA agreed to pick up the total cost of equipment, which would have tallied up toward $100,000, and even hinted at helping us with rent. It also helped that our friend who owned the space we were looking at was on the board of directors of the CRDA. Connections in business are invaluable. All we would have been responsible for was salaries. It would have given us a huge advantage right out of the gate.

Even with all the good things that we had lined up, Michelle wasn't exactly feeling Atlantic City. She was worried about safety. I couldn't argue with her, especially since most of the staff we'd be considering to bring onto the team were female. Michelle had a valid point. I even pitched hiring a security guard to be there early in the morning and late at night. She still wasn't in love with the idea, which devastated me after working so hard to make the possibility a reality.

We talked it out and agreed to look at other options for studio space. I eventually went to the CRDA president and told him we were shelving the Atlantic City studio idea. He was as disappointed as I was.

We continued to meet with potential investors and sponsors. The sponsorship proposition was an easy one. Nearly everyone we went to was all in. They were jumping at the chance to get involved and support a local program. We knew the sponsors would come easy. It was everything *else* that needed work.

Stockton University wanted to meet with us again to go over the terms of our contract. Michelle, Megan, and I went to their Galloway campus and met with several of their staff around a large oak table in a conference room next to their studio.

"We really love the idea of working with you and creating a program for our kids to learn, but after speaking with Comcast, it turns out that it just won't be an option," the director of the program told us.

"What do you mean Comcast won't let it happen?" I asked

"Technically, Comcast owns the channel we put our programming on. They will not let a third party come in and run ads on their space," she replied.

"Understood. I know what I have to do. Listen, I really appreciate you all wanting to make something work with us. Before we axe this plan, can you give me a couple weeks? I want to try meeting with someone who may be able to help on the Comcast end," I told her.

"Absolutely. We are here. We aren't going anywhere."

There they were—Comcast had struck again. Comcast had become the bane of my existence. An evil corporation trying their best to hinder the little guy who was just trying to make a difference in the local area.

We walked out of the meeting feeling defeated. I looked at Michelle and Megan and said, "Well . . . that's not what I wanted to hear. But I think I've got a plan."

"Of course you have a plan—why would I think otherwise?" Megan responded.

"What do you think we should do next? I mean, I think being able to broadcast our product on that channel is a game changer," Michelle added.

"Van Drew. I'm going to reach out to Allison and see if she can arrange a meeting with Jeff," I told them.

"Ohhh, that's a good idea. Let's try it," Megan said.

Jeff Van Drew was our newly elected congressman. We'd had a good relationship with him and his office since our days at NBC40. He was a big supporter of local news and understood the importance of having us on the air for local coverage.

I sent out an email to Allison, Jeff's chief of staff, that night.

Hi Allison! Hope all is well. I'm working on building a new TV station in our area. As you know SNJ Today closed down, and we are trying to get the ball rolling on something new. We have sponsors already committed to the project, but we are having issues with Comcast. I'd love to be able to enlist your help. Would you be able to set up a meeting with the congressman? Even a half hour of his time would be appreciated. Thanks!

Within fifteen minutes, I got a response.

Hey Nick! We've been following along to see what was next. Yes. I can absolutely do that. How does next Tuesday at 3 PM work? Our office here in Mays Landing good for you?

Mission accomplished.

It was obvious that one of our, if not our biggest, challenges was navigating the relationship with Comcast, the major cable provider in the area. We knew that for our station to gain traction, we'd need their support or at least their cooperation. To that end, we arranged a meeting with the one person in power who could have some influence over them. Normally a meeting with your congressman would be a formal affair complete with nerves and all, but we all knew Congressman Van Drew, and it was like going to chat with an old friend.

We presented our case passionately, explaining how this station wasn't just a business venture but a community necessity. The congressman listened attentively, offering advice and even suggesting potential introductions within the industry. After learning of our failed attempt to work with Stockton, he was intrigued. He told us he was going to give his contact at Comcast a call and see what he could do. While no immediate solutions emerged from that meeting, it underscored the importance of having political allies who understood the value of local media.

To formalize our efforts, we created a legal entity to house the new station. The founding group included myself; Michelle; her husband, Dean, who had several years of business consulting experience; and Megan. Each of us brought different skills and perspectives to the table, and initially, the collaboration felt promising. However, as I would later discover, the structure of the organization wasn't what it seemed. Unbeknownst to me, only Michelle and Dean, who were married, were legally listed as owners of the entity. This revelation would become a critical turning point in the journey.

Six months after SNJ Today's doors closed, the viability of SJN-TV was still very much up in the air. We had all worked on different things such as studio space, advertising agreements, potential employees, set design, and a list of equipment, but the financial reality began to set in. Michelle and Dean approached me during a meeting with a proposal that caught me off guard. They suggested pooling the revenue I was generating under the weather division to help sustain the station until it was fully operational. While I understood the financial pressures we faced, this proposal felt misaligned with the original vision and the work I had poured into building the weather brand.

The weather division had always been my passion. It was a niche I had cultivated, building trust and a loyal audience. Diverting its revenue felt like diluting its potential and jeopardizing its growth. After careful consideration, I made one of the toughest decisions of my career: to sever ties with the new station and focus solely on weather. I wished Michelle and Dean well. They are great people and their hearts were in the right place, but it became obvious after almost a year of working on the endeavor that this would not be a viable situation for anyone involved.

Walking away wasn't easy. I had invested countless hours, built relationships, and poured my heart into this dream. But the decision to go my own way felt like reclaiming my agency and doubling down on what I truly believed in. I restructured the weather division, investing in new technology and expanding our services to better meet the needs of our audience. It wasn't just about forecasts anymore; it was about providing hyperlocal, actionable insights that people could rely on.

As I watched the digital station, which became known as The Thread, launch in a different version than we'd imagined without me, I felt a mix of pride and relief. Pride that the vision had materialized, and relief that I had stayed true to myself and my goals. I didn't immediately have a name for my company but broadcasted under the "Nor'Easter Nick" umbrella—a brand that hundreds of thousands of people in South Jersey had already known. The weather broadcasting business was flourishing, becoming a trusted resource for the community and a testament to the power of focus and determination.

Looking back, the journey from SNJ Today's final days to building something new was both exhilarating and exhausting. It was a chapter filled with lessons about collaboration, trust, and the importance of knowing when to pivot. While the partnership with Michelle, Dean, and Megan didn't pan out as I had hoped, it taught me invaluable lessons about clarity and communication in business relationships.

Today, my company NorCast Media continues to carry the spirit of SNJ Today—its commitment to community, its dedication to storytelling—in everything I do. To me it is much more than a business; it's a way of giving back to the region that shaped me, just as SNJ Today once did. And while the paths may have diverged, the legacy of that journey remains a source of inspiration and a reminder of what's possible when you dare to dream big.

High temperature: 73°F **Low temperature:** 59°F
Conditions: Breezy with overcast skies and a clearing line on the horizon

Today reminded me of the transition zone between two air masses–turbulent, uncertain, and full of pressure gradients. Like launching a new venture after the collapse of another, these moments are tough to navigate but necessary to bring clarity and growth.

Sometimes, the warm front doesn't quite clear the clouds right away–but that doesn't mean the sun isn't coming.

–Nick's weather journal

Chapter Twenty-Two

FORECAST: LOVE

Amazing weekend on tap! Plenty of sunshine to go 'round, We will see highs in the 70s with low humidity. Take every opportunity possible to sit back, relax, and enjoy!

—Nick's Facebook Broadcast

A lot of people I know or have met seem to rush into life-altering decisions. I'm not, nor have I ever been, one of those people. I like to make sure everything is set in stone 1,000 percent before committing to anything that is going to impact me long term.

Brandon and I had been dating for three full years before marriage even entered my thought process. We had been living together for two and a half years and pretty much figured out each other's strengths, weaknesses, and flaws. We bickered here and there like any normal couple does, but there were no red flags for either of us. We were in a good place.

We went on a vacation to Hawaii the previous summer, and while there we picked out matching promise rings made from koa wood, so I knew what his ring size was. It was the sneaky way of getting what I needed when the time was right.

I knew he was my soulmate—my forever person. We had that feeling very early on in our relationship, so after three years it only felt natural. Why *not* take that next step? The very thought of that was 100 percent contradictory to everything I'd ever openly said. I never in a million years thought I'd get married. I'd always been somewhat afraid of commitment.

But here I was, about to make a life-altering decision and start a new chapter of our lives. I was ready. Did he feel the same way? I guess I'd have to wait and find out.

We planned a weekend trip to the Poconos. We had gone there on one of our first trips together early in our relationship, so it held a special place of significance in my heart. We visited Camelbeach Waterpark, did tons of hiking, and ended it with the 100 Mile View. I had done all those things many times as a kid, as my best friend's grandparents lived up there and I'd always go with him to visit them—so I was well acquainted with the area. It was one of my favorite places to go.

The first time we went together, Brandon loved it—especially the view from high atop the valley. On a clear day you can see about a hundred miles in all directions because you're standing at about five thousand feet in elevation. The plants, the wildlife, and the overall vibe are amazing, so I chose that spot to propose.

We packed the car, and with our dog, Skye, in the back seat, we were on our way. I went over in my mind a million times how things were going to play out. I checked my pocket another million times to make sure the ring was still there. Luckily everything was on track.

It was Skye's first adventure out of the area, so we were thrilled to get her on the hiking trails. Our first stop was Boulder Field, a must-see, unique area that was formed by moving glaciers during the Ice Age. As a science geek, I love everything about it.

After spending a couple hours hiking the various trails, we were getting closer to the 100 Mile View. My palms started sweating as my anxiety ticked up. All I could think about was: *What if he's not ready?* I couldn't shake that thought. Brandon is a few years younger than me. I didn't want to steal his early twenties from him, but we had such a good relationship—it wasn't like he was going anywhere. At the time he was twenty-two and I was twenty-five.

We got to the top of the hill, took in the tranquility while holding each other's hand, and held Skye close. It was a perfect ending to a perfect day. We walked another couple hundred feet to get as close to the edge as possible, within a safe distance.

It was now or never. I got down on one knee, pulled out the ring, and looked deep into Brandon's eyes.

"I am absolutely in love with you and want to spend the rest of my life with you. Will you marry me?"

There were a few moments of silence, which made me worry instantly. Brandon's eyes became teary.

"Yes. Of course I will!" he finally said. I breathed a huge sigh of relief, got up off my knee, and we embraced for a good five minutes before walking back to the car.

The whole moment was magical, and the day played out exactly as I had imagined. We both spent the entire trip home texting friends and family and formulating the wording for our social media announcement.

We weren't in a rush to actually *get* married, as we agreed two years would be a good period of time. We wanted to save as much money as possible to be able to do it the right way.

The next two years were spent picking out our suits, tasting cakes, and thinking about every possible detail. Brandon is the planner and details person. I just don't have the attention span for it. He basically gives me options, I give him my opinion, and then he chooses what he thinks is best anyway.

Planning was exciting. After all, we were prepping for the biggest day of our lives!

High temperature: 73°F **Low temperature:** 49°F
Conditions: Clear skies with unlimited visibility

Today, we stood at elevation with a view that stretched for miles—just like love when it's true and steady. The air was calm, the sky cloudless, and everything felt in sync. Sometimes, clarity in the atmosphere mirrors clarity in life. When you know, you know.

—Nick's weather journal

Chapter Twenty-Three

TORNADO OF GRIEF

Good morning, my friends! We've got a GREAT holiday weekend in store for us. Amazing beach weather with high pressure dominating through Monday. Fireworks? BBQs? Pool parties? All of those things will be good to go with highs in the 90s and lower humidity.

—Nick's Facebook broadcast the Friday before the Fourth of July

My little brother, Matt, and I had a very tenuous, at best, relationship. We didn't get to see each other a whole lot, but when we were kids and actually did get to hang out, we were a lot closer than we were during our teenage years. He surrounded himself with kids who I thought were a bad influence and pulling him down.

On top of that, our relationship suffered because of our mother's favoritism. He could do no wrong in her eyes. He was Jesus incarnate to her. He was *the* definition of a mama's boy. It irked me to no end.

Through high school we grew apart. He had his circle of friends who were entrenched in the party scene, and I had my circle who were the complete opposite. He cared less and less for school and more about hanging with his boys. Before I knew it, he was selling weed. That just pushed me away more, and it got to a point where I wouldn't even give him the time of day.

He was a smart kid. Brilliant even. But he didn't use those abilities for good. Instead he enjoyed being a bad kid. If he had only focused on school, he likely wouldn't have run into the issues he did. I think a lot of his problems came from teachers comparing the two of us. I was that stereotypical geeky "teacher's pet" and he, well, was not. I think they were expecting a repeat of me and were disappointed when they learned we were nothing alike.

The final straw for me was when he sold my car from under me one day. I had come home from a long day at work and wanted to take a nap. I left my keys in the car, like I usually did, because we lived in a very safe area, and I wasn't worried about crime—plus there was nothing in my car to take anyway.

I woke up, looked out the window, and saw my car was not in its parking spot. Within moments I realized it was most likely sold so my brother could get drug money. I loved that car. I got into an accident with it two years prior, and because I didn't have a penny to my name, I rebuilt it on my own by going to junkyards across the area. I had a connection to that car.

After that day, I hadn't spoken to my brother for a few years. I found out he moved on from marijuana and got into pills and heroin. I can't say I was surprised given the caliber of the people he was hanging out with. I've seen this story many times. Addiction runs in my family.

In 2017 Matt hit rock bottom. He had a near-death experience as he overdosed but was able to be revived. He sought me out for help, showing up at my house one night. I was surprised to see him since we hadn't had any communication in a very long time. He wanted to make amends and move on. He also wanted me to help him get into a rehab facility so he could straighten his life out.

I did admire his ability to admit he had made mistakes and was making strides to fix those mistakes. He had a plan to get a job selling solar panels lined up but wanted to get totally clean first. He roped me in. I agreed to help him, and within just a few months he was on track to be successful. He looked good, his skin had cleared up, he'd put on some weight so he didn't look like the wind would blow him over, and he had started working again.

I was proud of the progress he was making. Watching him turn his life around in such a short period of time made me feel good. I was hopeful for his future. I helped him pick out a place in Ventnor, and he was living on his own. He did very well for a good year, and then after a night out with his high school friends, he relapsed. I was angry and upset for him because he seemed like he just threw it all away.

He sank right back into the lifestyle I helped him get out of. I cut off communication with him again, and I hadn't heard from him again for almost a year when I got a Facebook message from him one night asking me how I was doing. He apologized for putting me through his issues. He asked me to help him through rehab one more time and swore up and down he was cutting ties with his friends and he wanted to get clean again.

I did it. I wanted to see the best for him. Even though we weren't close, he was still my blood brother. I felt like it was the right thing to do, plus I felt like I had a moral obligation to help. Just like the last time, he sobered up in a few months, we got him a job selling cars, and he was in a safe, stable environment on his own. He was doing well. We stayed in regular communication for the next year or so before he cut it off.

I stopped hearing from him out of the blue, and I got concerned after a few weeks. I called my father one night to see if he knew what was going on. What he told me disappointed me again. Turns out Matt had ended up back on heroin and was hanging out with the same vagrants that got him hooked from the start.

It was early July. Brandon and I were getting ready to go to Rehoboth

Beach in Delaware with some friends. Neither of us had ever been there, so we were looking forward to going down for the holiday. We were running late, as is typically the case for one reason or another, so I didn't notice my phone ringing. When I got into the car, I saw Matt had left a voicemail.

"Yo, Bro. It's Matt. I know you don't want to hear from me but I need your help. I'm serious. I want to get clean. This is the last time I'll ever ask you for help. I promise. Please help me out this time. Call me back."

I didn't feel like talking to him on the phone so I opted to send him a text.

"Matt—I helped you twice. Both times you did really good and then you fell right back into the same lifestyle you were trying to escape. I'm not doing it anymore. I'm sorry." Sent.

I didn't get a response, but that was typical, so I thought nothing of it. He'd get over it and come back to talk to me in another six months; I was sure of it. Brandon and I went about our day taking the trip about an hour south to Cape May, and then we boarded the ferry for another hour. It was a peaceful ride.

We met up with our friends once we crossed the bay, and we had dinner. This weekend was going to be different as we all rented an entire house. So many firsts! We had a blast our first night.

The next morning I woke up and saw a missed call from my uncle at 3:30 AM. That was odd.

"Nick, your brother passed away last night. Overdose. I thought you'd want to know. Give me a call when you can."

I stood there in shock. So many thoughts raced through my mind. I couldn't believe I was hearing those words. He had such a bright future, and he threw it all away, for what? I couldn't help but blame myself in some way for his death. *What if?* always came across my mind. *What if I helped him that final time—would he still be with us?*

When Brandon woke up, he could tell something was really wrong without even asking me.

"What happened?" he asked as he gave me a hug.

"Matt's dead," I told him.

He didn't say another word. He didn't have to. He was there with me in that moment and that's all I needed.

This was only the second time someone's death impacted me personally. This one stung more than my grandmother's passing because, well, she was in her nineties by that time, and she had lived an incredible life. Matt was only twenty-six. A baby. So much life ahead of him.

I still think about him often. I think about the good times we had when we were kids—and there were a lot of them. I think about staying up late at night, hanging out on the dock out back at my grandmother's, looking up into the void of space talking about crazy conspiracies and how we pictured life in the future. I think about how things might have been different if I'd stepped up and was closer to him in high school instead of just writing him off.

None of these things go through your head until you experience a tragedy of that magnitude. It will never escape me that the very last memory I have of Matt is him begging for me to help one more time—and I turned my back. Whether right or wrong, that will weigh on me for the rest of my life.

At my wedding we left two empty seats with pictures of him and my grandmother with plates and candles in hopes they'd both be there in spirit.

High temperature: 88°F **Low temperature:** 69°F
Conditions: Clear skies, humid, still

Today felt too still. Not a leaf moved, not a breeze in sight—just heavy, humid air covering everything like a weighted blanket. It reminded me of how grief feels when it first hits—no movement, no release, just pressure on your chest and a mind racing with memories you can't change. It's wild how you can feel both overwhelmed and numb at the same time. I thought a lot about Matt today. About that voicemail. About how final silence can be. The sky was so blue it almost felt wrong—like the weather didn't get the memo that the world had changed. Maybe it's just how it goes. The sun keeps rising even when it feels like everything else has stopped.

—Nick's weather journal

Chapter Twenty-Four

ANCHORED IN LOVE

A pretty large storm will ride through on the jet stream late tonight into tomorrow. We are talking high winds with gusts over 50 mph, 1"+ of rain, and maybe even some thunder and lightning.

—Nick's broadcast

There was a period of roughly six months in mid and late 2019 when things were in flux. Ken owned a small radio station that broadcasted under the call letters WSNJ. Ken kept me on to work in a part-time capacity, but that certainly wasn't enough to live on. I was slowly but gradually building clients that wanted to advertise on my platform. I had to come up with a price sheet and packages I could offer.

All of this was happening as I was preparing to get married. Talk about upheaval before a major life event, right? We both worked at the television station, so with its closing we lost two incomes and had to scramble to figure things out.

For the first time in my life I had to think about applying for unemployment. I knew I was entitled to it, but it still felt wrong. After all,

I had been working since I was a kid. Maybe it was an ego thing; I couldn't come around to admitting that I needed help for the first time in my life.

My business idea was in its infancy stages, so I wanted to make sure I had some cushion for at least a few months before I went full throttle and lost the safety net altogether. I did the deed. I applied. Within a few days I received a letter in the mail requesting I visit the local unemployment office in Pleasantville. They teach folks how to write résumés and prepare for an interview. I needed none of that. I met one of the counselors who greeted me with a big smile. He did his best to go through the motions while I nodded along. He offered me suggestions for careers.

Of course, I didn't need any of those suggestions because I knew exactly where I was going. I had a plan. I just needed that temporary helping hand to make sure all of my bills were taken care of. I didn't want to come across as rude; the guy was extremely pleasant and just doing his job. I thanked him for his time and I was on my way. The entire unemployment process is digital these days, so it made it quite easy to take advantage of the benefits. Within just a couple months I stopped because business was finally picking up, and I was confident about where we were headed. I didn't need to rely on the government any longer, as I knew we were going to be OK.

In the months following the closing of the Digital and Television sectors of SNJ Today, things got super busy. Wedding planning was a lot. We had to figure out venue, food, suits, and most important of all—who was invited to the wedding. It's amazing how stressful these situations are! I think the part that gave me the most anxiety was the guest list. Combined, we know hundreds of people. We've got a circle of "closer friends" of at least sixty. Add in their plus ones and families? Yikes! That's *a lot* of people. We didn't have the funds to do an extravagant wedding with two hundred people. Brandon's mother helped us a bit, but I certainly didn't have any help from my side of the family; they've got nothing to help with.

We had to be creative and as frugal as possible. We started going through our list of connections. We got ideas from friends and family. One of the best ideas—and ultimately what we would end up settling on as the style of wedding—came from our friends Sue and Laura, who are affectionately called "The Fishin' Chicks."

"How about a brunch wedding?" they suggested as we chatted over a meal at their cozy home in Ventnor.

Brandon and I looked at each other as if a lightbulb went off inside our heads at the same time.

"What an incredible idea!" I said.

Sue and Laura were always levelheaded and genuine in their recommendations. At the time we had only known them for less than a year, but we knew instantly that they were good people. Our friendship started when we met them for the first time at a fishing pier heading into Ocean City, a small shore resort about twenty minutes from where we lived. They were both avid weather fans and Facebook followers. They invited us to go fishing, and we hit it off immediately.

They told us that they had a brunch wedding and loved every moment of it—and it's less expensive than a traditional dinner wedding. We were on board immediately. We just had to figure out where we were going to have it. I went through the Rolodex in my head and thought about Resorts in Atlantic City. Resorts is the original casino in Atlantic City. It's been there for decades and has a certain charm about it. We also absolutely love the food at Capriccio. It's an Italian dinner restaurant, but they have an amazing brunch buffet that we've been to many times. When I realized that I'd known the events director at Resorts for a few years from working with our television stations, it was a no-brainer that it was worth reaching out.

I shot him an email telling him my idea for a brunch wedding, and he got back to me within a couple days wanting to set up a meeting. We agreed to meet that next weekend and have brunch at Capriccio. It was nice to reconnect with Dan; I hadn't seen him in a while. We went over the particulars—we gave him our ideas and he gave us his. We decided on a beach ceremony with the reception in one of their newly renovated event spaces upstairs. It sounded perfect in every way. A beach wedding was perfect for the kid who grew up on the beach. While everything sounded incredible, I was nervous about the price. I had a number in my mind, but surely it was way too low. We couldn't possibly get all those things—for a hundred guests, no less—for the price I was thinking, right?

If my Jewish grandmother taught me anything in life, it was how to be a shrewd businessperson.

Dan asked, "How does one hundred dollars a person sound to you?"

Now, ordinarily, anyone in their right mind would jump all over that. Everything we wanted for ten grand? We could get it done with minimal debt—but I wanted no debt. I looked him straight in the eye, and without even thinking it through, said, "I was thinking more like fifty dollars a person, and I will advertise the whole wedding on my Facebook page, photos and all."

Dan thought it over for a moment, looked back at me, and said, "We've got a deal!"

My tactics worked?! Wow! Even I was surprised. Our dream wedding for five grand. We could absolutely swing that.

The venue was set. Our next step was suits. I had no worries in that department because I had a guy—Dan Moroni—a custom tailor who to this day does my entire professional wardrobe. We opted for powder-blue tuxes. These weren't your ordinary tuxes though. Since it was a beach wedding and in early August, we didn't want to sweat to death. We went with blazers and shorts. It was different, but it worked! To complement the powder-blue threads, we chose a beautiful coral-orange for bow ties and pocket squares. We made sure to get the suits finished as quickly as possible so that we could put that part of it to bed early. I think we had everything done by April or May with plenty of time for any alterations.

The last thing we needed to secure was our cake. Not sure where to go since there were many bakeshops in our area, I took to Facebook to ask my viewers. We must have had two dozen people rant and rave about The Bake Works, a local place in Northfield. I reached out to set up a tasting and we loved it. Since it was a summer wedding, we wanted something light and airy. We settled on a lemon cake with buttercream icing. It was amazing. It was also another trade deal. I did a highlight of their business, posted it to Facebook, and gave them a hundred-dollar tip. All parties were happy, and we got a quality cake that everyone enjoyed. After walking out of the bakery, everything was set in motion, and we only had a few more things to tie up before the big day.

I'm going to be honest. Brandon did so much more to prepare for our wedding than I did. It's not even close. It makes sense, though, since he is the planner. I had say in the final decisions obviously, but most of the ideas were his, and he was on point from the very beginning. I had complete confidence in his ideas and his taste for different things. As hard as I try, I don't think I'll ever be the planning type, so I'm very thankful for him in so many ways. He picked out our "Save-the-dates," invitations, and décor that would go on the tables.

To save money, we went to Michaels and bought supplies so we could make the centerpieces. Much cheaper than buying pieces already assembled.

As the big day approached, excitement continued to build. This was a big step. Ten years prior, I never saw myself making such a commitment. I was a loner, a renegade. How did this happen? Love, I guess. Regardless of my prior thoughts on the subject, I was really looking forward to it.

It was exciting thinking about all the adventures we were going to take together. Even more exciting to think I'd finally found someone I meshed well with.

Several weeks before the wedding, we had brunch at Capriccio with our good friends Don and his husband, Louis. Don Guardian was the mayor of Atlantic City and told me several years prior that he wanted to be the one to marry us. As soon as we picked a date for the wedding, I contacted Don and asked him to be our officiant. We both love Don, so he was the perfect choice for the ceremony. He knew us well, we were comfortable with him, and he was part of our circle of friends in Atlantic City. A win-win. Neither Brandon nor I are religious people, so we wanted more of a quick, fun ceremony. A few months prior I was my best friend's best man for his Catholic wedding. Wow, are they long. I didn't want to put our friends or, frankly, us through something like that.

The big day was here. The venue was set, we had our room, the cake was being delivered, and the Resorts staff was working on putting everything together.

Brandon and I had a disagreement the night before. Want to know what we were arguing about? The weather. Yup. The weather. Oh, the irony, right? We had an option for a tent in the contract. It was an extra $500. I didn't think we'd need the tent, but Brandon came barging into the room showing me, of all things, his weather app that had a 30 percent chance of rain the next morning. I looked at him in utter disappointment and said, "Are you serious right now? You know how much I hate those apps. They're never right and HELLO! Weatherman here." He rebutted, "But what if it's right? What if it does rain? Everything is going to be ruined."

I guess it was victory number one for him because I ended up texting the events director to get the tent. I was extremely confident it wasn't going to rain. I was ready to die on that hill, but I was there to celebrate our wedding and not attend my funeral should rain happen. The next morning came. A beautiful sunrise greeted us to start the day off on a positive note. I woke Brandon up and walked him over to the window to see the view of the beach where we were about to get hitched in a few hours. "Wow! Look at *all* that rain out there. Man, I don't know if we should go through with it. It's really nasty out there. Maybe we should cancel because the rain is coming down so hard."

He looked at me like he wanted to push me off the balcony.

Our friends started arriving one by one. My future mother-in-law stood at the entryway to the beach waiting for us, looking as beautiful as ever. Brandon had several members of his family attend. It was wonderful. As for my family? No one. My own mother didn't show up to support me on one of the biggest days of my life. It still hurts a little, even today. I think back on it and wish I had a better relationship with her, but I've come to accept that it is what it is. It would have been nice to have her there, but you can't change the past. It's done and over with.

I think the most frustrating part of it is this: I sent an invite over to the house. She had it. She knew when the wedding was. She mustn't have shared it with anyone because my father didn't even know when it was, and he told me after the fact that he was upset that he wasn't there. It's that kind of stuff that has prevented me from developing a meaningful relationship with her—but I try. I try to mend some of the wounds of the past, but I'm not very successful at doing so. At any rate, it was great to see so many friends there because I've learned over the years that friends take the role of family, so, in turn, I had tons of family there that day.

I hate to admit this—don't tell Brandon I told you this, OK? Pinky promise? We ended up needing the tent. Not because it rained but because it was too hot! The tent worked out well to blunt the impact of the strong August sun. It was also as humid as all heck! The ceremony was everything we could have asked for. It was jovial, meaningful, and, most importantly, quick! Don was amazing and made us feel as comfortable as possible. As public a person as I am, I don't like tons of attention. I find it awkward to be standing in a place where everyone is looking at me. But Don was in charge and used his humor to break the ice and put us all at ease.

We exchanged our vows, said I do, and we were on our way to starting our next chapter together as a married couple. We went to Cancun for our honeymoon. It was the first time we had ever been abroad, and we had a blast.

At the time, we were living with friends, Paul and Mike, but knew it was time to buy our own place and leave the area we grew up in. We liked the Camden/Gloucester County region and were ready to take the big step into homeownership. Used to apartments and shared spaces, having a place of our own felt huge. We started searching on Zillow, contacted a few local realtors, and began touring homes.

Is it crazy to say that we found our home in one day? We visited maybe eight to ten homes, and the last one of the day was the one we wanted. It was a cute "Sears model" home tucked away in a small neighborhood in Blackwood, situated about twenty minutes east of Philadelphia. Was it our dream home? Nope, but it was a good start. Somewhere we saw ourselves living for five years. A place to call ours and invest some time and money into making it represent us. The house was yellow with a reddish roof and a green door. It was adorable. A little dated on the outside, but we saw the potential and leapt on it.

It was nice having a place to invite friends over to visit. We met new people almost immediately. We hosted board game nights, dinners, and small parties quite frequently. We loved that little house. I think it was just a few months into living there when we decided to expand our family. No—I'm not talking about children. As much as I like visiting schools and teaching and interacting with kids, I just don't think our crazy lifestyle would be optimal for raising them—for now. We are all over the place all the time, and I wouldn't want to neglect them in any way. I'm talking about another dog!

We had adopted our first dog, Skye, in 2016. While she was technically a "rescue," I don't really consider that to be the case since she was part of an adorable litter of puppies and would be grabbed up in an instant, but I'm happy we were able to get her since she's been my companion for all these years. Since we are so active, she would sit at home for long periods of time and be alone, which made us upset. We always talked about getting another dog so she'd have company. I am a big believer in going to shelters. There are so many good dogs out there that need loving homes. Every dog I've had has been a shelter dog.

We lucked out on our first trip. We walked into the Voorhees Animal Orphanage and saw several dogs that I was interested in, but one in particular grabbed Brandon's attention. He called me over to see this tiny Boston terrier shaking in a gigantic cage. While I was pulling for a dog a few cages down that looked like Skye, my heart still melted when meeting this little guy. From what the staff told us, he was a "frequent flyer." His story made it obvious that we just had to go with him. He was abandoned by his family, which I found heartbreaking.

After introducing him to Skye the next day, we adopted him when we found out they were compatible. We've now had him for four years and enjoy every moment with him. He's a bit rambunctious at times, but he's been an awesome addition to our small family—and we know that Skye enjoys the company when we are away! The two have continued to bond and are basically inseparable. I don't think we will ever be without two dogs; it's been a great experience.

We settled into our little close-knit neighborhood quickly. It was a 1940s-era blue-collar community. Everyone was friendly for the most part. We had the most amazing neighbors right next door. Donna and Joe introduced themselves to us the very first day we moved in and offered us anything and everything we needed. Having never owned a home before, we weren't totally prepared for the myriad of small issues that would randomly appear. If I needed a tool or advice on how to fix something, Joe was there! They are some of the most genuine people I've ever come across and they're so appreciated. They were even more appreciated when the pandemic hit.

By late 2019, I felt as though business was starting to pick up. I had a handful of advertising clients, our bills were paid, and I was doing what I loved. One of the main priorities I had when we were looking for a home to buy was building a TV studio. Up until the point of being homeowners, I always had a makeshift setup. At the place we lived prior, I set up a camera and a couple lights and stood in front of a sixty-five-inch television. Before that, I had a green screen in the dining room. Those methods worked but didn't give off the professional look that I was going for.

Our new home had a basement. Great! There was enough room to build what I wanted. There was one issue though—it was an unfinished basement. There are times severe weather happens in the middle of the night and I must jump out of bed and cover it live. Truth be told, I was creeped out as hell going down those creaking steps. There were exposed pipes, electrical wires, and a covered drain in the floor where I imagined the girl from *The Ring* was going to emerge and get me. There were also spider crickets that would randomly show up. I had no idea what they were until one jumped on my leg in the middle of live storm coverage one night. I almost had a heart attack.

From the viewer's standpoint, though, it worked. The product looked great on the air, and that's all I cared about. For the first couple weeks I had my desk and computer equipment in the basement, but that got old really quick. I opted to move everything to the second story of the house and wire things down to the basement. I was much more comfortable being in an actual room. I only had to spend the time it took to record my weather forecasts in the basement. The rest of the day was upstairs, which was a relief!

High temperature: 88°F **Low temperature:** 70°F
Conditions: Hot and humid with a few clouds and a light breeze

Today reminded me that sometimes we plan for rain and get sunshine—and other times, we prepare for sun and get heat waves. But either way, we adjust, we adapt, and we keep moving forward. Just like building a home or starting a life with someone, weathering the unexpected is what makes the story worth telling.

—Nick's weather journal

Chapter Twenty-Five

FORECASTING FROM HOME

Well, guys, we are looking at some hot and sticky weather overall with dew points climbing into the 70s. Not good if you have any work to do in, say, a basement. Trust me on that one!

—Nick's Facebook broadcast

Moving into our new home in Blackwood was a dream come true—a blank canvas ready to be transformed into something personal, meaningful, and entirely ours. We dove into renovations right away: new roof, fresh siding, energy-efficient windows, and a lush backyard. But the crown jewel of all these projects wasn't visible from the outside. It lived beneath our feet—our soon-to-be full-scale television studio.

From the very beginning, I had a clear vision. The basement would become more than just a workspace; it would be a broadcast hub that could rival commercial studios. Instead of focusing on traditional creature comforts, we poured our energy into functionality and tech. The transformation began with designing the space to handle the demands of a high-end production environment.

We installed professional-grade LED panel lights on ceiling mounts for consistent, studio-quality illumination. Brandon custom built the green screen—meticulously measured, painted, and paired with low-reflective wall paint to reduce spill and shadows. But what really elevated the space was the tech stack.

We brought in 4K broadcast cameras with motorized lenses for smooth pans and zooms, all routed into a TriCaster-style studio switcher that allowed real-time scene transitions, lower-thirds (titles), and live streaming across multiple platforms. The switcher software gave me full control of every broadcast element—camera feeds, graphics, chroma-key overlays (this is how the green screen works), you name it—all from one command station that was set up to be completely automated—controlled by hot keys on my clicker.

The acquisition of SNJ Today's Baron weather graphics system was a game changer. Originally a $60,000 setup, I secured it for a fraction of that cost. With it came access to high-resolution radar data, forecast models, and customizable animations that made every weathercast look like it came straight out of a major-market newsroom.

We set up soundproofing panels to reduce echo and built a dedicated editing suite adjacent to the main studio. From recording to post-production, I could produce a complete segment—forecast to final cut—in just a few moments, which was great because I didn't want to spend more time in the basement than I had to. Thankfully, my actual office where I spent most of my time was upstairs. The environment was fast, efficient, and built for performance. For the first time, I wasn't just matching the quality of bigger stations—I was exceeding it in some ways.

Of course, the process wasn't without challenges. Wiring the studio was an exercise in patience. Routing power, Ethernet, HDMI, and audio lines while maintaining airflow and minimizing interference required hours of planning. But watching it all come to life—the smooth transitions between scenes, the crisp audio, the flawless green-screen keying—made it more than worth it.

This studio became my creative command center. A place where I could control every aspect of production, from forecast maps to lighting cues. It became a symbol of what's possible when you dream big and get your hands dirty turning vision into reality.

What started as an unfinished lower level became the heartbeat of the house. Not just a room with equipment, but a living, breathing ecosystem where storytelling, technology, and passion intersected every day. Our home in Blackwood wasn't just renovated—it was redefined.

High temperature: 74°F **Low temperature:** 52°F
Conditions: Sunny with a calm breeze

Today I watched the sun rise through a layer of morning haze, casting soft beams through the windows of my new basement studio. The air outside was still, but down here, things were humming—literally. The switcher fans, the camera gears, the buzz of LED panels warming up. It reminded me of a quiet weather day—stable, reliable, yet filled with potential energy. That's what this studio represents: a high-pressure system of creativity and control.

Sometimes we wait for the right forecast. Other times, we build the environment ourselves.

—Nick's weather journal

Chapter Twenty-Six

BACK TO THE GREEN SCREEN

We've been in a bit of a rut for the past ten days or so, but that looks to change as we press into midweek. Highs will be much more seasonable, climbing into the 70s!

—Nick's Facebook weather broadcast

One day, out of the blue, I got a phone call. It was a 973 number, which meant it was coming from North Jersey. I rarely ever answer the phone. I always let it go to voicemail so I can filter the call.

I forgot about the call for a few hours and then ended up checking into it. A man named Lee Leddy from a media group based out of Freehold was searching for a weatherman for their planned television newscast.

Oh boy. Here we go again, I thought. While I liked the position we were in at the moment and saw a lot of opportunity for growth, I still wanted to hear him out and learn where this was going and where I could possibly fit into the equation.

I picked up the phone, just before five in the afternoon, and dialed the number. Lee answered almost instantly. He gave me some background on what they were trying to do and requested to meet with me in person the following Monday. It sounded like a fun project, so I was excited to meet him and learn more.

On Monday, I plugged the address into my GPS and was on my way up the turnpike to US 130. It was just over an hour away, but the trip seemed to go quickly since most of the time I was in seventy-mile-per-hour traffic.

I got a little turned around when I pulled into the complex. There must have been a hundred different offices—and they all looked exactly the same. After circling the parking lot for about ten minutes, I found an SUV lettered ME-TV2. That had to be the place.

I walked in and was greeted by the secretary, whom I told I was there for a meeting with Mr. Leddy. She instructed me to take a seat and assured me that he'd be with me shortly.

As a full-on TV geek, I couldn't stop my eyes from bouncing around the room. Old TV station promo posters were all over the place; multiple awards and tons of artifacts from a bygone era dotted the walls. It was a fascinating place to see in person.

Within a few minutes, a cheerful man with Al Roker–like glasses stepped into the waiting room and introduced himself as Lee Leddy, the general manager. We walked back to his office and got off to a great start.

"We are going to do something that hasn't been attempted before, and we want you to help us," Lee said.

Right off the bat, my interest was piqued. "What do you mean, exactly?" I shot back.

He went on to explain that New Jersey is a TV news desert, and no media company has dedicated resources to covering the things that matter for the eight or so million people who call the state home.

This was all stuff I had already known, but would the circumstances really change? Was this man about to tell me they had a plan to transform the landscape of local news? It was nearly the exact plan we had at SNJ Today, and we all know how that turned out.

"We've built the studio, we have the equipment, we have the business model hashed out, and now we are hiring the people who will be the face of the newscast," he went on.

"We are going to cover the entire state. From Hunterdon County to Cape May County, we want to make sure everyone is served," he told me, smiling cheek to cheek.

What an ambitious goal, I said to myself.

He asked me about my experience and background. He was happy to know I had almost a decade of television experience under my belt.

I've always been one to drive a hard bargain. Different thoughts raced through my mind—chiefly the idea of having to commute over an hour into North Jersey. During rush hour? That would be a nightmare. I had a TV studio built at my house. What if I were to take advantage of that? It was worth asking, right? After all, the answer is *always* no if you don't ask.

I cleared my throat and spoke up after a pause in our conversation. "Mr. Leddy, this all sounds very interesting to me, and I would love to be a part of it, but the commute isn't very appealing. I have a TV studio at my house. What if I used that and we tapped into the signal at the station? I have the same tech you guys have here, and it would be a benefit to you because I could pay even more attention to the weather and be on top of it a little better rather than sitting in traffic."

He looked at me like I had just spoken French to him.

"Let me get this straight. You have a TV studio . . . in your home?" he asked.

"Yes, sir. I've been trying to build my own business and have been broadcasting local weather to South Jersey residents on my Facebook page. It's worked out very well."

He looked intrigued by my answer. He put his right hand up to his chin and thought for a few minutes before replying. "Alright, if you think it will work, I've got no problem with it. I just need to have our tech guys check out everything."

By the end of the conversation, he gave me a number. He told me to think on it and get in touch with him in a few days.

I didn't have to think about it for a single moment. He was offering me a salary of $65,000, full benefits, work from home, and allowing me to keep working on my business on the side? It was a no-brainer.

I told him I accepted the offer on the spot and could get to working on graphics and our overall look immediately. We shook hands, he told me to be on the lookout for a contract in my email in the coming days, and he took me for a tour of the newsroom and TV studio before we parted ways.

I couldn't wait to get back into the car to call Brandon and tell him what just happened.

I was the happiest I had been in years.

This was probably the best opportunity of my life outside of the initial job offer at TV40 that got me into the field. Brandon was very excited by the news, and the whole car ride home, all I could think about was the position we were going to be in within a few short months.

Having a steady salary and working from home (before it was cool) was amazing.

On top of that, having the flexibility to keep the customers I had and continue to grow my business in South Jersey was incredible.

I was over the moon by the time I got home.

Good things do happen to people who put the time and energy into what they love.

I am very grateful for Lee and the PMCM-TV team. They really gave me the huge kick-start that I needed. The job with them allowed me to expand my exposure to my audience and build my business at the same time. It was a dream scenario. I was allowed to work from home and not required to travel an hour and a half from South Jersey to Freehold every day. They also let me explore sponsorship opportunities for my Facebook page that would lay the foundation for my business going forward.

Since it only took me a few hours a day to fulfill all my obligations for them, I spent a ton of time meeting with local business owners and securing financial stability.

High temperature: 73°F **Low temperature:** 55°F
Conditions: Breezy with building clouds

Today reminded me of a "pressure gradient"—the tighter it is, the stronger the winds. Life's the same way: The more pressure you're under, the faster you move . . . but it doesn't have to be chaos. Sometimes, those winds shift just right and carry you exactly where you were meant to go.

—Nick's weather journal

Chapter Twenty-Seven

CLOUDS OF UNCERTAINTY

We've got areas of heavy rain moving in from the south—
not that it matters because we are all stuck inside anyway.
Look for 1 to 2" of rain before the end of the day.
—Nick's ME-TV2 broadcast

One afternoon in early 2020, I stood in the middle of my basement studio—tea in one hand, mic cable in the other—staring into the green glow of the weather wall. Outside, the world had hit pause. Inside, my small corner of it was surging forward.

A virus had brought everything to a halt. Schools shut down. Offices went dark. Highways emptied. But screens? They lit up like never before.

Everyone was online. Everyone was hungry—for answers, for connection, for comfort. Suddenly, people who once laughed at social media as "just for kids" were relying on it to know whether to send their kids to school, mask up, or even go outside. The digital space became the new living room, newsroom, and classroom—rolled into one.

It felt like the world stopped spinning, but my career sped up.

I had been posting local weather updates on Facebook for years, mostly for my South Jersey followers. Sometimes a couple hundred people watched. On snow days, maybe a few thousand. But now, tens of thousands were tuning in. Parents. Teachers. Mayors. First responders. My inbox turned into a constant scroll of questions and gratitude.

"Can I send my staff in tomorrow?"

"What time will the storm hit?"

"Thank you. You're the only one talking to us."

Information became oxygen, and I was doing everything I could to keep it flowing.

And here's the truth: I was scared too. Just like everyone else. I was disinfecting groceries, Googling "symptoms of COVID-19" every night, and worried sick about how we'd pay the bills. But when the camera light turned red, I pushed that aside and gave people what I could—clarity. Confidence. Calm.

That's the thing about crisis. It doesn't care if you're ready. It doesn't wait for the perfect moment. It just shows up, uninvited—and you either crumble or create. I chose to create.

Brandon and I were still living in our first home. I was in the process of rewiring the house—quite literally—to expand my broadcast reach. It wasn't glamorous, but still, it worked.

From that gritty, concrete room, we built something beautiful. My social platform turned into a trusted news source. I developed sponsorship packages. Local businesses started calling me—not just for ads, but for help.

"How do we get the word out that we're open?"

"Can you spotlight us?"

"Can you make us matter?"

I said yes. To every single one.

Because it wasn't just about weather anymore. It was about being seen in a world that felt invisible.

In a time when national news was focused on chaos and fear, I focused on community. I started a segment highlighting small businesses. I showcased families safely trick-or-treating. I told stories of recovery. Of reopening. Of resilience. My page became more than a forecast. It became a hub. A heartbeat.

Looking back, I realize the world wasn't just shifting. It was transforming.

Local news wasn't dying—it was being reborn online.

People didn't stop caring about their communities. They just stopped finding value in traditional outlets that overlooked them. What they needed was someone they knew, who understood where they lived, who could be a likable "Poindexter" and walk them through whatever Mother Nature had up her sleeve. The human connection is the most valuable aspect of what we do.

So I became that person.

By the time the world started turning again, I wasn't the same. None of us were. But instead of rebuilding what I had, I doubled down on what I created.

The pandemic taught me that connection doesn't come from a fancy studio or a satellite truck. It comes from honesty. From consistency. From showing up.

And that's what I still do—every day. From the same studio that started as a basement broadcast experiment, now fully built out, now streaming to tens of thousands.

The world changed. I changed. But the mission didn't: Keep people informed. Keep them safe. And always—always—meet them where they are.

Even if that's in a comment section at 1 AM.

High temperature: 73°F **Low temperature:** 50°F
Conditions: Calm with high, thin cirrus clouds drifting eastward

Today, I broadcast the weather from the same basement studio that has been a work in progress since before the pandemic—where I learned that connection isn't about fancy equipment; it's about showing up when people need it most. During COVID, we were all isolated but united in uncertainty. Just like those thin cirrus clouds that stretch across the sky ahead of a warm front, the tension was quiet but constant. And yet, through the cloud cover of fear, I saw how light—information, truth, community—still broke through. That's when I knew digital platforms weren't just the future of news . . . they were the now.

—Nick's weather journal

Chapter Twenty-Eight

NorCast IS BORN

We've got a major break in the pattern. Something new and fresh as the storm track eases up and high pressure builds in. This pattern looks to hang on for a while.

—Nick's Facebook broadcast

It was the height of the COVID-19 pandemic, a time when the world felt like it had been flipped on its head. People were stuck at home, businesses were closing their doors, and uncertainty loomed over every aspect of life. Amid all the chaos, I found myself in a unique position. My social media broadcast company was starting to take off. I had been building my brand, known as "Nor'Easter Nick," for years, and now, people were tuning in to my broadcasts for reliable and engaging weather updates. The demand for hyperlocal, accessible, and relatable information was skyrocketing, and I was right there to fill the gap.

Yet, despite the momentum, my company still didn't have an official name. It was more of an extension of my personal brand than a distinct entity. "Nor'Easter Nick" was recognizable, but I knew that if I wanted to grow and make a lasting impact, I needed something more. However, finding the right name—one that encapsulated both my vision and the essence of what I was building—was easier said than done.

Then came my husband. Brandon was a bright, creative, and driven young man who had a knack for thinking outside the box. One day, he approached me with an idea. He was working on a final project for one of his classes and wanted my help. The assignment? Create something educational and impactful. Brandon's idea was to teach kids how different types of weather formed through an online video series. It was a brilliant concept, especially at a time when kids were stuck at home, parents were desperate for engaging educational content, and digital learning was becoming the new norm.

"Nick," he said, "I think we could do something really cool here. We can make it fun, interactive, and easy to understand. Imagine kids logging on and watching videos where you break down the science of weather in a way they actually enjoy. We could call it 'NorCast Weather School.'"

I paused, letting the name sink in. "NorCast?" I repeated.

"Yeah," Brandon said, his eyes lighting up. "'Nor' from your nickname, Nor'Easter Nick, and 'Cast' because, you know, everything in digital media has 'cast' in the name. It's perfect!"

It was a lightbulb moment. NorCast. Simple, catchy, and meaningful. It tied back to my personal brand while also feeling fresh and professional. The name immediately resonated with me.

We dove headfirst into the project. Brandon and I brainstormed topics that kids would find fascinating—thunderstorms, tornadoes, snowstorms, hurricanes, and even the science behind sunny days. I wrote scripts, drew diagrams, and put together visual aids that would make the complex concepts of meteorology accessible and fun. Brandon handled the production side, bringing his youthful energy and technical know-how to the table.

The first episode of "NorCast Weather School" focused on thunderstorms. I explained how warm air rises, cools, and condenses to form clouds, which then grow into the towering cumulonimbus structures that produce rain, lightning, and thunder. We added animations, sound effects, and even a few jokes to keep things lively. By the time the video was edited and uploaded, we couldn't wait to see how it would be received.

To our delight, the response was overwhelmingly positive. Parents flooded my inbox with messages of gratitude. Teachers reached out to tell us how they were using the videos in their virtual classrooms. Kids were sending in their weather questions, curious and eager to learn more. What had started as a school project quickly became something much bigger. "NorCast Weather School" wasn't just a hit—it was a phenomenon.

After we wrapped up the initial series, Brandon and I sat down to reflect on what we'd created. We were both exhausted but exhilarated.

"You know," I said, leaning back in my chair, "I think we've stumbled onto something here. NorCast . . . it's not just a name for the weather school. It could be the name for everything. My entire company."

Brandon nodded. "Absolutely. It's clean, it's professional, and it's still tied to you. We should rebrand everything as NorCast."

And that's exactly what we did. Over the next few weeks, I poured myself into the rebranding effort. "Nor'Easter Nick" wasn't going away, but it was evolving into something bigger. NorCast Weather became the new face of my broadcasts, my social media presence, and my growing business. The name felt like a declaration: This wasn't just a personal brand anymore. This was a company with a vision, a mission, and a purpose.

The rebranding process wasn't without its challenges. We had to redesign logos, update social media profiles, and explain the change to my audience. But every step of the way, I was fueled by the excitement of what NorCast could become. The new name gave me clarity and direction. It was a brand that could grow with me, encompassing not just weather forecasting but also other ventures I dreamed of pursuing in the future.

As NorCast Weather took shape, so did my aspirations for the company. I envisioned it as more than just a source for weather updates. I wanted it to be a hub for education, innovation, and community engagement. The success of NorCast Weather School proved that we could make an impact beyond traditional forecasting. We could inspire curiosity, foster learning, and connect with people in meaningful ways.

Looking back, it's amazing to think about how it all came together. The pandemic was a time of uncertainty and fear, but it also forced me to adapt, innovate, and think creatively. Brandon's school project was the catalyst, but the journey of NorCast was about so much more than that. It was about seizing an opportunity, embracing change, and building something that could stand the test of time.

The broadcast landscape is changing fast and furious. We are seeing companies who own multiple television stations consolidating their resources, creating weather "hubs" that are used to produce forecasts for markets hundreds of miles away, and seeing mass layoffs. It's clear we can no longer say "digital is the future"; it's now "digital is here and now."

Today, NorCast is a name that people recognize and trust. It's a brand that started in the midst of a global crisis but has grown into something resilient and enduring. And every time I see the NorCast logo or hear someone mention the name, I'm reminded of the moment it all began—when two people sat down to create a video series for kids and ended up laying the foundation for something extraordinary.

I've been in close contact with several meteorologists across the country that are well known in their home markets and have left traditional television to create a replica of my business in New Jersey. Together it is our goal to expand on what I've built to create a National

Weather Network. It is the next logical step on our way to revolutionizing our field.

High temperature: 81°F **Low temperature:** 60°F
Conditions: Breezy with increasing sunshine

Today reminded me of a clearing cold front—when the clouds break, the winds shift, and you feel that first breath of fresh air. That's exactly how launching NorCast felt. In the middle of the storm that was COVID-19, Brandon and I found a pocket of calm and built something lasting. Like naming a high-pressure system that clears the skies, finding the right name brought clarity and momentum to everything that followed.

Sometimes, when the atmosphere is unstable, it only takes one lift—one spark—to set everything into motion.

—Nick's weather journal

Chapter Twenty-Nine

WEATHERING NEW HEIGHTS

A HUGE disruption to the pattern is incoming as the Madden Julian Oscillation goes into Phase 8 (cold). That will be the catalyst behind some significant changes. Out with the old and in with the new—buckle up!

—Nick's Facebook broadcast

Six years. As of this writing, that's how long I've been building this digital media business, and it's been a ride unlike any other. Along the way, I've learned invaluable lessons—what to do, what not to do, and how to pivot when things don't go as planned. I've also built some remarkable relationships, both professional and personal. Many of my advertising partners have stuck with me since day one, and others have joined more recently, bringing fresh energy and unwavering support. These partnerships have turned into friendships that I deeply cherish, and they've played a vital role in the growth of the company.

I still find it hard to believe how much the company has grown. What started as a simple idea—weather broadcasts from my basement—has transformed into a national media powerhouse. It's humbling to reflect on the journey from those modest beginnings to where we stand today. A pivotal moment came in 2022, when I made the bold decision to purchase a weather consulting company called Neoweather, based in Ohio. Until that point, I had no experience in weather consulting. But when an opportunity presents itself, sometimes you have to leap and trust your instincts.

Weather consulting delivers precise, hyperlocal forecasts tailored to the needs of municipal governments, contractors, landscapers, and entertainment venues. By working with independent weather experts, organizations avoid relying on generic weather apps—and save significant money in the process.

Take this example: An app might say it'll be 31° with snow possible. A township could then spend hundreds of thousands prepping roads—salting, brining, mobilizing crews. But if the snow doesn't come or the temps stay too warm, that effort (and cost) is wasted.

That's where human intelligence comes in. A weather consulting team analyzes the exact location, interprets multiple forecast variables, and delivers a confident recommendation: "Stand down, no action needed."

It's not just a forecast—it's a strategic advantage.

Neoweather was the brainchild of two entrepreneurs, Brian Ivey and Mark Spencer, who had reached a crossroads in their partnership. They were planning to dissolve the company into a larger entity and walk away. However, when I met with them, I saw potential. After some negotiation, I bought out Mark's share of the company and purchased 1 percent from Brian, making me the majority owner. Brian came out to New Jersey that October, and we spent the weekend mapping out the future of the business. Over dinner, we discussed how rebranding

Neoweather to NorCast Consulting could diversify our offerings and strengthen the NorCast brand.

Rebranding was just the beginning. To this day, the consulting side of the company remains a challenge. Salaries and overhead costs are high, and profitability has been elusive. However, with the help of our general manager, Jeff Mendelson, we're working tirelessly to turn it into a sustainable and profitable part of the business. It's a slow process, but I believe in the long-term vision and the team we've built.

In August 2023, we expanded further by launching a video production company under the NorCast umbrella. This venture, NorCast Productions, was spearheaded by Brandon, who had spent time as a talented marketing director, working with some of my clients. Brandon wasn't passionate about traditional marketing, but he excelled at video production and storytelling. We both agreed it was the right time for him to take the lead on this new project. Since its inception, NorCast Productions has attracted a diverse client base, from local businesses to large corporations, and it's quickly becoming one of our most exciting ventures.

By the summer of 2024, we added yet another branch to the NorCast family: NorCast Marketing. This social media marketing company was a logical next step, leveraging my name recognition to offer competitive services to local businesses. By undercutting the competition while delivering high-quality results, NorCast Marketing has become a profitable enterprise, helping our clients manage their online presence effectively.

Today, NorCast employs nearly two dozen talented individuals who are passionate about their work. Together, we're projected to generate a million dollars in revenue this year—a milestone that fills me with immense pride. Reflecting on how far we've come, I'm reminded of my rough start in life and the struggles that shaped me. Building this media empire hasn't been easy, but it's been worth every challenge. From weather forecasts in my basement to a multifaceted media company, this journey has been nothing short of extraordinary.

I am never satisfied with the status quo. I am always looking to move on to the next thing and figure out ways we can expand our footprint and impact to the community and the industry writ large. Sometimes it is difficult for me to stay still. Our past go-to vacations were all-inclusive beach destinations. We haven't been to one in a long time; instead we opt for activity-packed European trips or cruises. I would find myself sitting on the beach very restless as my mind was going in a million different directions.

Brandon would always yell at me for bringing my laptop to the beach—I have to admit, while I've tried to *work on* that, it hasn't changed a whole lot. Some of my best ideas usually come when I'm away. I'm not sure what it is—maybe the change of scenery—but something invigorates my creativity, and I end up getting so much done. Major decisions we've made regarding the direction of the company have come on vacation. I guess I need to get away even more?

It's extremely important to have a work/life balance. There was a time earlier in my career when I was working eighty hours a week. That's just not sustainable. You will burn yourself out no matter how committed and resilient you may be. Working hard and keeping your nose to the ground and your mind focused is extremely important, obviously, but when you don't allow yourself to take a breather, it ends up being counterproductive, and you wind up holding yourself back—trust me. I've been there more than a few times.

Running your own business is totally different than working for a company. There are advantages and disadvantages, but I think the good outweighs the bad 1,000 percent. There is a constant pressure placed on your shoulders because the decisions you make not only impact your life and your immediate situation, both the financial and work balance, but also the lives of the people who work for you. If a big customer pulls out and ends the relationship, I have to scramble to figure out how to cover that lost revenue as soon as humanly possible so we don't go extended periods of time without a balanced budget.

What's really cool is this: When you work for someone, you are reliant on a yearly raise. That is pretty much your only opportunity to level up and make more money. If I want to make more, I will create a new product to sell to a prospective advertiser or client. We want to go on a dream vacation? Great—let me sell more ad space to cover the cost. This is a lesson for anyone who wants to get into business for themselves. The buck quite literally stops with you. You have every ability to grow without any ceiling, but you have to work hard for it.

My business model was the first of its kind in the United States, and I wear that as a badge of honor. The broadcast industry is dying, and what we do is no longer the future; it is the here and now. The reality of the situation is that folks simply do not wait until six in the evening to get their news and weather. They want it now. They want that information easily accessible 24/7—and we provide just that.

Between my Facebook page, website, mobile app, and streaming channel, we are reaching and engaging a couple million local residents a week. Our numbers are undoubtedly neck and neck with television stations in the Philadelphia market—and advertisers know that. It's why our model works so well. We offer clients an opportunity to get their message out to a captive audience that are actively looking for the information we provide and at a fraction of the cost they'd be paying on a traditional TV broadcast.

TV stations should have adopted this model, but the mega corporations that own them were far too shortsighted. They believed the TV industry was going to chug on for years without competition. The COVID era changed that. These mega media conglomerates are laying off high-salaried employees left and right. Sure, it helps with their high overhead problem, but most of the time the people they let go are the very personalities who had a connection with their audience and kept them coming back. As unfamiliar faces take those jobs, the audience dwindles—and so, too, do the ratings and ad revenue.

Our original goal was to provide broadcast-quality content that folks have become accustomed to seeing on television and deliver it through a digital-only medium. We've achieved that goal. Now we are constantly working on the monetization aspect of what we do. On the weather broadcast side of things, we are filled to the brim. The challenge is figuring out how to upsell customers or create packages that include products from our marketing and production divisions, and when it makes sense, from the consulting company.

We are a very unique business that provides a ton of different services with the idea of keeping everything in-house for our customers front and center. We got our start with mom-and-pop stores and are now working with medium and large companies that are looking to hand off all their marketing to a third party. There are obviously many other companies that do the same thing in the game but they don't have *me.* The "Nor'Easter Nick" brand has become very valuable, and we use it to bolster the sales of the other branches of our company.

I also make sure we are always in touch with our local roots. It's imperative that no matter how big you get, you never forget where you came from. Big corporations that provide the same services we do are impersonal. They don't care about the business. They care about cashing that check every month and finding other businesses that will fall for their shady tactics. We want to be helpful, transparent, and work with our clients as partners.

The goalposts are always moving. How far do I want to go? I don't know the answer to that question at the moment. I suppose I want Nor-Cast to be the biggest name in weather. There's a lot of work ahead of us, but we are on the right footing to make a major impact on the industry.

We are constantly looking to bring other well-known personalities into the fold and replicate our model in markets all over the country.

It's kinda like the David and Goliath story. Goliath in this case is Comcast. None of this would exist today as it does if Comcast didn't shut down NBC40 or block us from being on a cable channel with SNJ Today. I've made it a point to be as successful as possible because of the flak we got from them early on. Comcast is now in the rearview mirror, and they have absolutely no control over the trajectory of my company, and I love that. Sometimes you need a major event with a perceived foe to give you the motivation you may otherwise not have had.

High temperature: 89°F **Low temperature:** 66°F
Conditions: Hazy sunshine with scattered cumulus clouds

Today reminded me of how small beginnings—like puffy cumulus clouds on a summer afternoon—can build into something much greater with the right energy and environment. Much like a growing thunderstorm, NorCast started as something small and localized. Now, it's become a multibranch media force—pushing upward, branching out, and expanding with intensity.

Momentum matters. Once a storm catches lift, it grows. So does a dream, if you keep fueling it.

—Nick's weather journal

Chapter Thirty

NETWORKING IN THE SKY

We've got a nice day on tap for the big chamber event on the beach tonight! Light wind, tons of sun, and comfy temps. If you're in the area, stop by. I'd love to see ya!

—Nick's Facebook broadcast

In the realm of television meteorology, connecting with your audience isn't just a skill; it's a lifeline. As a TV meteorologist, I've learned that building relationships with the people who trust you to inform, guide, and even comfort them during moments of uncertainty is one of the most vital aspects of the job. However, this emphasis on connections didn't start with my professional career; it has been a thread running through my life, shaping who I am and where I've landed today.

Growing up, I was fortunate to have teachers who recognized potential in me, even when I struggled to see it in myself. These mentors didn't just teach me subjects; they taught me resilience, discipline, and the value of striving to be the best version of myself. These relationships were foundational, providing a safe space to grow, learn, and dream. Their belief in my capabilities instilled a confidence that would prove invaluable in my future endeavors.

In my journey toward becoming a TV meteorologist, the art of connection began to take on a broader scope. It wasn't just about maintaining strong bonds with mentors; it became about creating new ones with people who held the keys to opportunities I hadn't even imagined yet.

One of the pivotal moments in my life came when I was welcomed into the circle of Rich Helfant, a man who ran Lucy the Elephant, the beloved gigantic pachyderm in Margate City, New Jersey. Rich's charisma and drive were infectious, and his guidance provided a blueprint for cultivating relationships with people who can open doors. It wasn't just Rich, though. Through him, I connected with Don Guardian, the mayor of Atlantic City at the time, who offered a different perspective on leadership, influence, and community service.

These relationships weren't built on convenience; they were built on mutual respect and shared goals. I learned early on that fostering these connections wasn't about what I could take but about what I could bring to the table. Whether it was lending a hand during an event or offering my expertise in weather to help plan community activities, these contributions solidified my place within these circles. The lesson? Relationships thrive when they are reciprocal.

In the world of business, these lessons took on new dimensions. Surrounding myself with people who had power, resources, and a wealth of experience was not only inspiring but strategic. When I transitioned into new ventures, I leaned on the friendships I had cultivated over the years. They became my sounding boards, my allies, and, at times, my champions. These individuals helped open doors to opportunities that might have otherwise remained inaccessible. In return, I offered them my loyalty, my work ethic, and my unwavering support.

One of the most critical aspects of developing these relationships is authenticity. People are drawn to those who are genuine, who show up as themselves without pretense. Whether it's an audience watching you on TV or a business associate considering a partnership, authenticity builds trust. And trust, in turn, strengthens connections.

In my field, connecting with an audience means more than just delivering the weather. It's about creating a relationship where viewers feel seen and understood. When I'm on-screen, I'm not just presenting a forecast; I'm speaking directly to someone who's planning their day, worrying about their family's safety, or simply seeking a friendly face amid the chaos of life. Those moments of connection are why people invite you into their homes, morning after morning, evening after evening. It's about consistency, reliability, and relatability.

So, how do you build and nurture these relationships, whether they're with your audience, mentors, or professional connections? Here are a few principles that have guided me:

1. **Be Present:** In every interaction, whether it's a casual conversation or a high-stakes meeting, being fully present shows the other person that you value their time and input. It's the foundation of meaningful connection.
2. **Offer Value:** Relationships flourish when both parties bring something to the table. Whether it's expertise, encouragement, or a shared vision, contributing meaningfully strengthens bonds.
3. **Show Gratitude:** A simple thank-you can go a long way. Acknowledging someone's role in your journey not only strengthens the connection but also reinforces your authenticity.
4. **Stay Consistent:** Just as viewers expect reliability from their meteorologist, consistency in relationships builds trust. Follow

through on promises, show up when you say you will, and maintain open lines of communication.

5. **Invest Time:** Building connections isn't a one-and-done deal. It requires ongoing effort. Regular check-ins, meaningful conversations, and shared experiences deepen relationships over time.

As I reflect on the connections I've made—from my teachers who encouraged me to aim high, to Rich Helfant and Don Guardian who welcomed me into their circles, to the audience who trusts me every day—it's clear that these relationships are more than just stepping stones. They are the foundation of my success and my happiness. They've taught me that when the right people are in your life, the possibilities are endless.

If you're looking to achieve your goals, whether in TV meteorology, business, or any other field, start by building connections. Seek out mentors who inspire you, friends who challenge you, and colleagues who support you. Be intentional about fostering these relationships and don't be afraid to invest time and energy into them. In return, you'll gain not only opportunities but also a network of people who believe in you and want to see you succeed.

Ultimately, connections are about more than professional success. They're about building a life rich in relationships that sustain, inspire, and empower you. And in the end, isn't that what truly matters?

High temperature: 84°F **Low temperature:** 61°F
Conditions: Calm with high pressure overhead

Today's atmosphere was quiet—stable and centered. It reminded me of the power of presence and connection, like a high-pressure system that brings clarity and calm. In weather, high pressure builds trust in the forecast; in life, strong relationships do the same. Whether it's your audience, mentors, or peers, when you nurture connection with consistency and authenticity, the storms ahead feel a little less daunting.

Good weather doesn't just happen—it's the result of balance, much like the relationships that shape our lives.

—Nick's weather journal

Chapter Thirty-One

WEATHER TIPS FOR LIFE

Well, folks, today will be a day to get up off the couch and immerse yourself in nature. It's gonna be a wonderful Wednesday with sunshine and blue skies as far as the eye can see! A walk or run? Get to it!

—Nick's Facebook broadcast

Life rarely serves success on a silver platter. For me, it's been a journey fraught with trials, tribulations, and lessons I'd never trade, no matter how painful they were in the moment.

I've shared glimpses of my childhood—how my grandmother, my rock, raised me. When dementia took hold of her mind, it wasn't just heartbreaking; it was life-changing. Overnight, I became her caretaker. I was a kid, forced to shoulder responsibilities most adults would struggle with. There were nights I'd cry myself to sleep from the exhaustion, fear, and weight of it all. And when she was gone, life didn't ease up. Moving in with my parents introduced a new kind of challenge—mental abuse that chipped away at my sense of self-worth. It was a time when escape felt like an impossible dream, and yet, I survived.

Later, the professional world presented its own hurdles. My career in TV began at seventeen, and I poured every ounce of myself into it. But the industry can be as ruthless as it is rewarding. I endured multiple station closures—each one a gut punch that made me question if I had a future in the field. And then there was the personal struggle of grappling with my identity. Coming to terms with being gay wasn't just about self-acceptance; it was about finding the courage to live authentically in a world that doesn't always welcome authenticity. The weight of hiding, the fear of rejection, and the journey to self-love were among the hardest battles I've fought.

Through it all, I've learned some truths I want to share. If you're reading this, no matter where you are in life, take these words to heart.

Turning Negativity into Power

Negativity is inevitable. People will doubt you, life will knock you down, and some days, it'll feel like the universe is conspiring against you. But here's the secret: You can use that negativity as fuel. Every insult, every failure, every rejection—take it and transform it into energy to push forward. Let it sharpen your resolve, not break your spirit. Negativity is only as powerful as you let it be.

Surround Yourself with Support

The company you keep can either lift you up or drag you down. I've had to learn the hard way that not everyone in your life wants to see you succeed. There are people who will root for your failure, whether out of envy, insecurity, or malice. Let them go. Life is too short to carry dead weight. Instead, surround yourself with people who genuinely want to see you thrive. Find those who inspire you, challenge you, and celebrate your victories as if they were their own.

Believe in Yourself

Self-belief isn't just a nice idea; it's a necessity. If you don't believe in yourself, how can you expect anyone else to? There were countless moments when I doubted I could endure, succeed, or even just keep going. But deep down, I clung to the belief that I was capable of more. That belief carried me through dark days and fueled my climb to brighter ones. Believe in your abilities, even when the world doesn't. Especially when the world doesn't.

Chase Your Dreams Relentlessly

Dreams often feel out of reach, and that's OK. The best ones usually are. But no matter how wild or improbable they seem, don't give up on them. I've seen my craziest aspirations come to life because I refused to stop trying. Success doesn't come overnight, and the path is rarely straight, but persistence is your greatest ally. Keep going. One step at a time, one day at a time.

Remember Your Roots

No matter how far you go in life, never forget where you started. My journey from that scared kid taking care of his grandmother to where I am today has been long, but I carry my roots with me. They ground me, remind me of why I started, and keep me focused on what truly matters. Success isn't just about where you end up; it's about staying connected to the experiences and values that shaped you.

Final Thoughts

Life isn't easy, and success doesn't come without sacrifice. But I promise you this: You are stronger than you think, more capable than you realize, and more deserving than you believe. Use your pain as a catalyst, your challenges as stepping stones, and your dreams as your guiding light. Surround yourself with love, positivity, and purpose. And most importantly, never stop believing in yourself. You have everything you need to achieve greatness. Now, go out and make it happen.

High temperature: 70°F **Low temperature:** 48°F
Conditions: Cloudy with clearing skies by evening

Sometimes storms roll in slowly—thick clouds, cold air, and darkness that lingers longer than you'd like. But no storm lasts forever. The sun always finds a way back.

Today reminded me that every challenge in life is like weather: unpredictable, intense, sometimes cruel—but temporary. What matters is how you face it, how you grow through it, and how you keep walking until the skies begin to clear.

—Nick's weather journal

Chapter Thirty-Two

SHADOWS OF THE PAST

It's February 2, Groundhog Day. I'm standing in a muddy field at five in the morning in Punxsutawney, Pennsylvania. For the uninitiated, the town celebration centers around a groundhog named Phil. According to tradition, if Phil emerges from his burrow and sees his shadow, there will be six more weeks of winter.

The ceremony takes place at Gobbler's Knob, a small hill. Though I've come to fulfill the promise Bebe and I made to each other to visit in person one day, disappointingly, the spot looks nothing like the movie we used to watch together. It is mostly a barren field with some trees in the middle of nowhere. There's no cute Main Street—none of it. In that sense, I'm glad my grandmother and I didn't make the trip when I was a kid after all.

Brandon's along for the day, helping with the camerawork and being an overall good sport. It's overcast and the ground is soggy from heavy rains the day before. The event seems sparsely attended, and I wonder if this is a sentimental waste of time. But here we are, and I wasn't going to leave without a broadcast.

I manage to find a patch of ground that I can stand in without slipping in the mud.

"How does it look on your end?" I ask him.

"Good backdrop. Good light," he says, setting up the camera and plugging into our live box. He gives me the one, two, three countdown with one hand in the air.

"Nor'Easter Nick here, broadcasting live from Punxsutawney, Pennsylvania . . ." I feel the mushy ground and barren landscape disappear. It's just me and my audience and the conditions I'm explaining to them.

After our live shot, we move closer to the stage to check out what's going on. We stand at the edge of a crowd of about 1,500 people waiting to see a member of the Punxsutawney Groundhog Club try to summon Phil from his burrow. This local dignitary is dressed in a tuxedo and top hat for the occasion.

"Nick, look behind us. Isn't that Jim Cantore?"

I turn. Brandon is right. There, about a hundred feet behind us, is my childhood idol from The Weather Channel!

A million thoughts rush to my mind. There's so much I want to say to him. That his weather forecasts helped turn a little boy scared of storms into a kid who looked forward to them. That he inspired me to learn and gave me hope for my future.

He is the reason I'm standing here today.

"You have to go say hi," Brandon says. My palms start sweating and my heart races. I haven't felt this nervous since my first broadcast back in 2010. I think about Bebe, and I know what she would want me to do.

So I walk up to weather icon Jim Cantore. But before I can introduce myself, he looks at me and says, "You're Nor'Easter Nick! I'm so happy to see you here. I've heard a lot."

I'm shocked that he knows who I am. It's an incredible moment. I just wish I could go back in time to tell my scared childhood self what awaited in the future.

Jim Cantore and I shake hands. One of the greatest meteorologists ever to step in front of a camera knows me—and he's a nice guy too!

I feel like I've finally made it. I'm grateful to have Brandon by my side to share the moment, but of course I can't help but wish Bebe were here with us. One day, I hope to see her again and tell her all about it.

That's a rain date I'm looking forward to.

High temperature: 39°F **Low temperature:** 31°F
Conditions: Overcast with soggy ground from previous rain

This morning, I stood on muddy ground in Punxsutawney to honor a promise I made long ago. While the field wasn't as magical as the movie, something else made it unforgettable—meeting Jim Cantore, the very meteorologist who once sparked my passion for weather.

Sometimes the skies may be gray, the ground unsteady—but moments like these remind me that no matter where you start, you can end up standing exactly where you once dreamed you'd be.

—Nick's weather journal

Acknowledgments

This book would never have come to fruition if it weren't for my amazing husband, Brandon Panter. He has been with me nearly every step of my career from the last year at TV40 to creating our business. He is always inspiring me in new ways to be the best version of myself as possible.

I'd like to thank Dr. Damiso Josey who guided me through high school and gave me the opportunity to practice what I love throughout the four years at Hammonton High.

My TV Media / English teacher Mr. Gary Joseph will always be someone I look up to and appreciate. If it weren't for his endless optimism and big-picture outlook on life, I'm not sure I'd be the person I am today.

Megan Wolf remains one of the most important people in my life. She started out as my boss but today she is one of my closest friends and confidants. She is there every day in any capacity I need her, whether it's business or personal.

A big thank-you to my agent, Adam Chromy from Movable Type Management, who took a chance on me and encouraged me to write the book. He also made valuable connections that I'll never forget.

Of course I'd be remiss if I didn't mention the team at Matt Holt Books. From Matt to Katie, everyone was a pleasure to work with.

About the Author

"Nor'Easter" Nick Pittman is the president, CEO, and founder of NorCast Media Group, a dynamic multimedia company that blends broadcast meteorology, consulting, production, and marketing. Nick's lifelong passion for weather was born out of fear—his childhood terror of severe storms evolved into curiosity, and eventually, a full-fledged career.

Raised in Brigantine, New Jersey, Nick experienced every type of coastal weather imaginable, from hurricanes to nor'easters. His broadcasting journey began in elementary school, delivering the daily weather on the morning announcements. By age seventeen, Nick became the youngest on-air weather forecaster in the country when he landed his first professional role at an NBC affiliate in Atlantic City.

After a decade in local TV, Nick launched NorCast in 2019. Under his leadership, the company has grown into a regional weather powerhouse with a team of four on-air meteorologists and eight support staff. Nick's work focuses on hyperlocal forecasting and community-first storytelling.

In 2018, he created the "Rainy Day Project," a charitable initiative dedicated to helping struggling families in South Jersey. To date, the project has raised over $100,000 and provided support to more than a thousand families.

Nick lives in Gloucester County with his husband, Brandon—his partner in life and in business—and their two dogs, Skye and Zeus. Together, they are building a brand grounded in authenticity, service, and heart.